WHAT'S YOUR ERA?

Sophie-May Williams

a celebration of
Taylor Swift

HarperCollins*Publishers*

This work has not been endorsed by Taylor Swift, but it is dedicated to the global pop icon who, for millions of people around the world, is considered to be their ultimate role model.

CONTENTS

INTRODUCTION

Taylor Alison Swift is a music phenomenon. She has been rightly described as the 'world's biggest pop star', whose popularity has reached stratospheric heights. She is a master storyteller, capable of weaving together complex and emotionally charged narratives, and her music focuses on a spiritual journey of self-discovery and self-acceptance.

Taylor inspires her fans to embrace their own journeys of self-discovery and growth, and die-hard Swifties, like myself, already feel intensely connected to her and her music. We feel a strong social and emotional bond with her brought on by highly relatable lyrics, which explore a raft of universal issues that then provide a link to our own identities.

She writes honestly and openly about vulnerable subjects such as her struggles with anxiety, body image and relationships. Taylor has written about the constant support she receives from her family and those close to her to follow her dreams, and why she is so curious about 'the way people treat each other'. She told *Elle UK*: 'I love writing songs because I love preserving memories, like putting a picture frame around a feeling you once had.'

Taylor is acutely aware that evolution is key if you want to remain relevant in the music industry, especially as a woman. Of course, there have been female trailblazers before, notably Madonna, Christina Aguilera and Britney Spears, who have all experienced dramatic image reinvention, but Taylor is considered the consummate skin shedder. Our inspirational heroine has successfully crystallised her evolution over the years, and I imagine Taylor sees life as one giant journey book, comprised of chapters, which open and close.

All Swifties will already be aware that these chapters are referred to as 'eras' in Taylor's world. Each of Taylor's albums and eras has a unique personality and reflects a progression of her sound, style and overall aesthetic. And each era is defined by its own 'personality', where Taylor has morphed and evolved. She even puts meaning behind every packaged aesthetic detail, from the design and fonts to her infamous hidden 'Easter eggs', which see her embed messages in liner notes, lyrics, music videos and even the outfits she wears. These references generate interest and discussion among her ever-growing community of fans, who collectively put on their Sherlock Holmes cap and cloak to figure out what Taylor's next move will be.

Cryptic clues aren't the only way Taylor interacts with her fans, though. She has a unique relationship with them and regards their loyalty, trust and happiness as being as important as the threads in a tapestry. After all, she doesn't view them as distant admirers gazing up at her from her pop-icon throne, but as friends who, like her, are navigating the ups and downs of life and are simply there alongside her for the ride. This egalitarianism is why we've stuck by her for all these years, from her social media exchanges to the listening parties she's hosted at her own home, where she invites fans to join her to listen to an album before its release. Most powerfully, over the past few years, Taylor has been reclaiming agency over her music through the re-recordings of her albums. Of course, Swifties had her back from the minute she announced she'd be rewriting her own history, as for many, it allowed us to relive our own.

It's Taylor's commitment to the cause, by virtually (and physically) bear-hugging her fans every single day, whether through her music or by posing her latest riddle, that keeps the cogs turning. It's her courage to speak up and recover what's rightfully hers, and pave the way for all those who are following in her footsteps – and will do later.

It's not an overstatement to call Taylor, *TIME Magazine*'s 2023 Person of the Year, an icon. After all, *TIME* editor-in-chief Sam Jacobs called the pop phenomenon 'the rare person who is both the writer and hero of her own story [and who has] found a way to transcend borders and be a source of light'.

Welcome to *What's Your Era?* It's been waiting for you ...

A love letter to Taylor

I'd like to think of myself as a multi-faceted Swiftie, but really, I think everyone is in some respect. Because, if we're being honest – regardless of whether you grew up listening to *Speak Now* or *1989* – you literally cannot tell me that you don't headbang to 'Better Than Revenge' in your bedroom. Or listen to 'Style' while deciding what to wear in the morning.

What's interesting – and genius – about Taylor Swift is that you can absolutely resonate with the era that cemented your status as a lifelong Swiftie, but you can also dip in and out of her other eras – and identify just as well – with a record that came out five years later. Not to mention the *slew* of other albums before, after and in between.

Think about it: you can be a *Fearless* gal during those nostalgia-soaked Sundays when you're listening to the soundtrack of your youth and remembering how it made you feel when you first heard it. Or, it's the perfect album to blast at full volume with your pals before a night out. Alternatively, it's a bit of *folklore* when the bohemian fairy princess in you decides to rear her head and dress like Fleetwood Mac's Stevie Nicks. However, if we're talking about the album that placed the Queen of Pop on your radar, and subsequently landed you on the never-ending Taylor train, what would it be? Because while everyone here clearly has an overwhelming love for the star, you all have your own reasons for being a Swiftie. Your own memories to treasure and reflect on. And your own emotions that are tied to your era for life.

For myself and a lot of other mid-Nineties babies out there, *Fearless* (2008) or *Speak Now* (2010) are pretty significant albums. Both were reasonably close in our teenage timeline and came out during the years when we can safely say we had zero life experience, but an overactive imagination. Back then, it was all too easy to daydream about what falling in love might feel like. Or what heartbreak could look like, too. Of course, what we envisioned was never quite the same as how things turned out, but until they actually happened, it was nice to believe that a first kiss could be 'flawless'. For that, Taylor, we'll always love you.

This book is mainly a big, fat, soppy thank-you to the queen herself for being with us from our teenage years all the way through to adulthood, and in doing so, effortlessly creating each iconic era.

For many of us, Taylor's music has been the soundtrack to some of our core memories, from first crushes to the first heart-wrenching break-up. From our first day of college to the last moment we pined over someone who didn't feel the same way ... It's easy to listen to a Taylor Swift track and be transported back to the very moments that shaped us into who we are today.

So let's take a deep dive into the Taylor Swift archives as I ask you the most important question of all: what's *your* era?

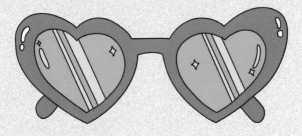

HOW TAYLOR ARE YOU?

Whether you're new to the Swiftie club or you're a seasoned veteran, you're all here for one reason: because you love Taylor Swift.

We could all learn some life lessons from Taylor, from how to be the ultimate best friend to how to follow your dreams and reach your full potential. So, if you're already on your way to becoming 'more Taylor' (i.e. you've mastered the art of friendship bracelets and you own more than one cat), or you need a little guidance on slaying your cottagecore style, this quiz can help point you in the right direction …

What item do you always carry around in your tan satchel?

A. Red lipstick
B. A parasol
C. Who needs a bag?

What do you think is your best quality?

A. Loyalty
B. Confidence
C. Being the life and soul of the party

What's holding you back from achieving your dreams?

A. Nothing! I'm an ambitious go-getter
B. Looking after my cats
C. My social life is too busy

If you were to have one pet, what would it be?

A. Just one? I need a whole tribe of kittens!

B. A cute Dachshund puppy

C. A koi fish – they're low-maintenance but still cute

Who would be your celebrity BFF?

A. Selena Gomez

B. Gigi Hadid

C. Miley Cyrus

If you could see anyone in concert – obviously, apart from Taylor – who would it be?

A. Haim

B. The National

C. Beyoncé

Mostly As

You couldn't be more like Taylor if you tried! You're always donning a red lip (because it's the best make-up statement anyone can make, duh), you're the loyal pal in your friendship group who's always there to give the best advice and you're ambitious in all the right ways. Keep going, sister, you'll crush those dreams eventually! Oh, and you're also the best kitten mama going, who loves nothing more than snuggling up with your furry friends after a long day's songwriting.

Mostly Bs

You're on your way to becoming just like Taylor, but you've still got a little way to go. Okay, you might think you're too busy looking after your cute little kitten to work on your goals and dreams, but it's all about balance. If there's something you really want in life, you've got to go out and grab it with both hands. You've still got exceptional music and girl squad taste that Taylor would approve of, though.

Mostly Cs

You really are the person everyone wants to hang out with at the party – I salute you, my friend! Being a social butterfly is a great trait, but you've still got some work to do if you want to be just like Taylor. Don't worry, though, a couple of songwriting sessions, a grande caramel non-fat latte a day and a friendship bracelet-making workshop will sort that right out!

1.

TAYLOR SWIFT

(2006)

Cast your mind back to 2006, specifically October. Taylor was in a studio in Nashville about to drop her debut album.

Simply titled *Taylor Swift*, this was a 16-year-old's first go at becoming a serious country artist. It was released only a year after she signed a six-album deal with Big Machine Records. Written while she was still in high school, little did Taylor know that those 11 songs would place her in the spotlight, where she would remain until this day.

Taylor stuck with what she knew and what she wanted to write about: her outlook on life as a teenager and how she dealt with relationships along with sweet narratives on friendships and how she navigated her insecurities. You know, just a pick 'n' mix of legitimate teenage worries and intrusive thoughts, with an extra peppering of sunshiney enthusiasm and optimism.

At the time, Taylor was sporting a cute country twang, which affirmed her early sweet girl-next-door vibe and acknowledged her love of country music – a key era-specific element. It also very much separates Taylor's early work from her later albums as the eventual softening of the country-esque feature allowed her albums to sound comparatively more mature.

Taylor is a credited writer on all of the album's tracks – a mean feat at just 16. The era was also the beginning of her relationship with songwriter Liz Rose, who would become a regular creative collaborator on her sophomore album, plus help her pen the now-iconic underdog track 'All Too Well' on her 2012 album, *Red*.

Upon the album's release, most critics were on board with the record, which was marketed as strictly country. It was Taylor's songwriting abilities, even though she was still a high-schooler, that were a standout element, which led to her winning Best New Artist and being nominated for Album of the Year and New

Vocalist of the Year at the 2008 Academy of Country Music Awards (ACM). On a bigger scale, the record ended up landing Taylor her first Grammy nomination for Best New Artist. (Her awards cabinet is now brimming with the golden accolades – 12, to be exact.)

Elsewhere, the track 'Our Song' gave Taylor her very first record-breaking moment: the youngest artist ever to have written and performed a Number-One track on the Hot Country Songs chart.

The accolades and achievements didn't stop there. *Taylor Swift* went on to spend a cool 24 weeks at Number One on the Top Country Albums chart. As for the *Billboard* 200? It peaked at Number Five. And by December 2009, just over two years after its release, the album had spent 157 weeks there. Not to mention it being the longest-charting album of the 2000s. As if that wasn't enough, it was certified Platinum in 2007.

This era saw Taylor start to perform her music on a bigger scale, being given the opportunity to open for already established country artists like Tim McGraw, Faith Hill and George Strait. Back then, her performance style was simple and understated. Just Taylor, her guitar and the ability to connect with and hold an audience, despite being a lot younger than the sea of concertgoers.

In terms of Taylor's marketing efforts and hustle to pull fans in during this era, she was well ahead of her time. The album was released back in the Myspace days, and thanks to artists like Lily Allen and Arctic Monkeys, the website was a popular research tool for finding new music. Back then, it wasn't really a space for country artists, nor their marketing strategies. Of course, that didn't bother Taylor, who decided to utilise the platform to grow her own community, and in doing so, she created an audience of young girls who were into country music, which was pretty much a non-existent demographic at the time.

What defines the era?

In a nutshell, the *Taylor Swift* album is Taylor's first era, her 'hello, this is me' introduction that placed her in the spotlight. It was also a sneak peek into her songwriting abilities, and it confirmed her desire to be seen as an artist, not just a singer. Taylor's autobiographical narratives, even as a 16-year-old, defined her songwriting.

Elsewhere, Taylor's debut came during a period when it was becoming cool and acceptable to like country music. (Not that anyone has the power to decide what's cool or uncool. As Taylor herself lives by and preaches, you should enjoy your guilty pleasures and be proud of them.) Timing also played a role for this album, as it dropped when female country artists like Carrie Underwood and LeAnn Rimes were experiencing a sudden surge in popularity. (Whether Taylor ignited the 'cool girl' country era is entirely your call.)

What's interesting about the debut is that some country experts, most notably in Nashville, still weren't convinced by Taylor as an artist at that point. They clearly weren't on the same page as those earlier music critics championing the album, such as from Chris Neal, Jeff Tamarkin, Nick Cristiano and even *Rolling Stone* ... Perhaps inherently fastened in their beliefs that country music *shouldn't* be synonymous with teenage angst and first-date flutters, many deemed Taylor's efforts as inappropriate and irrelevant to the genre's then-key demographic: the middle-aged.

Taylor's musical middle finger to the haters is another key feature worthy of mention in her debut era. Why? Because it proved she was prepared to stick it to the man, self-advocate for her talents and essentially stomp her cowboy-boot-laden feet and let people know that she wasn't going anywhere anytime soon. And that she was prepared to prove herself as a serious artist, despite her 1989 birthdate.

While majorly and squarely country in all the right places, the album's hints of pop laid the groundwork for Taylor's subsequent country-pop crossover. At points, it just *feels* like she's going to whip off those cowboy boots and whack on those heels. Taylor's first era helped her to successfully create an image that heralded her both as 'the next big thing' and 'the girl next door'.

Taylor Swift outfit inspiration

If you've got debut Taylor on the brain for your next Swiftie event, there are a few things you're going to need to aim for in terms of wardrobe, hair and make-up. The following items and looks are non-negotiables for achieving the 2006 country-chic Taylor:

TIGHT, BOUNCY CURLS
(you'll need a pair of really good curlers).

COWBOY BOOTS

SUNDRESSES – a white frill cotton dress is a must.

BOHO JEWELLERY – dreamcatcher-style earrings, beaded bracelets.

A Y2K THICK DISC WESTERN BELT IN BROWN/TAN

Now you've got the whole country-girl-meets-boho essentials down, in comes the fun bit: actually styling the whole look. If you're going for a white cotton dress you can pair it with the feather earrings plus a wrist full of beaded bracelets. It's important not to go too overboard on the jewellery here: boho accessories are statement pieces within themselves, remember. Naturally, you'll want to pop on a pair of cowboy boots – tan or gold are preferred.

You don't have to wear a white dress, by the way. Whether that's for fear of spilling your drink all down it while dancing or simply because it's not your colour. Taylor's debut era also featured plenty of other country boho styles, including ruffled asymmetrical halters with paisley patterns and floral summer dresses. Taylor's 'Tim McGraw' debut single artwork is a great point of reference for the latter.

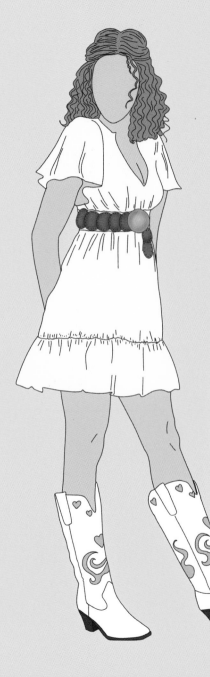

13

ALBUM STATS AND ACCOLADES
Taylor Swift (Debut)
Release Date:
24 October 2006
Debut on *Billboard* 200:
Number 19
***Rolling Stone* Rating:** 3/5
Certified (RIAA):
Seven x Platinum

2.

FEARLESS

(2008)

Taylor Swift circa 2008 was on a mission. Following the immense success of her debut album – plus the sudden rush, excitement and whirlwind that is newfound fame – an 18-year-old Taylor was inherently set on her path towards world domination.

Once again, Taylor penned every single song on her second record, *Fearless*, along with the talent of other co-writers like Liz Rose, John Rich, Hillary Lindsey and Colbie Caillat, a Grammy-award-winning American singer-songwriter whom Taylor hugely admired. The two also ended up duetting on the song 'Breathe'. This was a big win considering that Taylor at this point was considered an up-and-comer, while Colbie Caillat was an established and well-respected name in the music industry, with a large group of dedicated fans.

The success of Taylor's debut album had generated great interest in her as a musician and performer. It's also true that she recognised the importance of collaborations early in her career but was now in a position to call upon some of the industry's biggest names, who, recognising her talent early on, were just as eager to work with Taylor. But songwriting-wise, even though she had access to award-winning talent, Taylor wrote the majority of the tracks all by herself. 'Love Story' has become one of her most famous singles to date, and it went on to win a string of prestigious awards, including Song of the Year at the Country Awards in 2009 and the Pop Awards in 2010.

'Love Story's beginning is just as interesting as 'Fearless' itself. Taylor wrote 'Love Story' in just 20 minutes on her bedroom floor. According to fan folklore, she was feeling too inspired to leave the track unfinished and couldn't leave until she'd written the shell of what became a pop hit. This highlights Taylor's passion, motivation and ambition as a songwriter.

These days, old-school Swifties have an extensive, layered and nostalgic relationship with the track. For many of us, 'Love Story' isn't just a pop song about a metaphorical troubled Romeo and Juliet romance, it also encapsulates the long-lasting relationship between Taylor and her audience. Think about the opening lines of being young when we first saw her, closing our eyes and the flashback starting there. Forget the song's actual narrative – those words penetrate *deep* when *Fearless*-era fans think about how long ago their Taylor journey began.

As well as Taylor being an author on the majority of the tracks, she also co-produced the whole album alongside Nathan Chapman, the man behind a number of Taylor's other records.

Fearless saw Taylor add some more obvious folk and pop influences into her music, which were the first clear signs of her efforts to eventually cross over into pop territory, which music critics were also quick to recognise. It's elements like these where you can start to see the subsequent evolution and transformation in terms of her career.

Jon Caramanica of the *New York Times* even said:

'She has quickly established herself as the most remarkable country music breakthrough artist of the decade. In part, that's because she is one of Nashville's most exciting songwriters, with a chirpy, exuberant voice ...

'Most important, though, she very much sees country music as part of the larger pop panorama. A huge success on country radio, she has also found homes on pop stations and at MTV. Put more plainly, she has proved that there's no reason a country singer can't be a pop star too.'

The incredibly crafted songs, the attention to detail, plus the bolder, more confident attitude act as Taylor's reincarnation from a cutesy country gal into the eventual Grammy-winning pop icon we now see before us.

While we're talking about Grammys – and the evidence to prove Taylor's stratospheric career ascent – *Fearless* won Album of the Year (her first time winning this accolade) and Best Country Album at the 2010 awards. It was also Taylor's first time performing at the ceremony, where she duetted her song 'Fifteen' alongside an equally young Miley Cyrus. The performance was so wholesome – just the two of them, who were great friends at the time thanks to bonding as young starlets in the pop world, sitting on a podium amid a sea of important industry heads.

Her first win simultaneously landed Taylor a place in the history books as the youngest ever artist, at that time, to claim the category, at 20 years old.

In 2009, *Fearless* won the same prize at the Country Music Association Awards (CMAs) and the Academy of Country Music Awards (ACMs). The track 'White Horse' was also widely acknowledged, with Taylor nabbing two more Grammys for Best Female Country Vocal Performance and Best Country Song.

It was Taylor's *Fearless* era that catapulted her into world-tour territory. From 2009 to 2010, she promoted the album with the *Fearless Tour*, which was her first ever headlining concert tour. Visiting North America, the UK, Australia, Japan, Canada and the Bahamas, it grossed over $66 million and was attended by an estimated 1.2 million people.

As a sign of her growing stardom, her staging was far more complex than previous live performances, from production to costume changes. This set the tone for all future tours she would embark on, which only got bigger and better with each album. Oh, and Justin Bieber was one of Taylor's supporting acts after she invited him to tour with her!

Fearless was also when Taylor began to sprinkle her now-expected Easter eggs into her songs, albums and record packaging. For her, hiding secret messages, hints, clues and teasers in her content were other ways to keep fans on their toes while strengthening the sense of community within her world. Classic *Fearless* Easter eggs include Taylor capitalising the letters that spelt out 'I CRIED WHILE RECORDING THIS' for the song 'Fifteen'.

When it comes to the general themes of *Fearless*, Taylor did stick to the teenage narrative reminiscent of her debut. After all, she was a teenager herself. Still exploring the realms of romance, heartache and ambition, the difference between the *Taylor Swift* and *Fearless* eras was that the album took on more of an imaginative journey, with Taylor using metaphorical and descriptive language when writing her lyrics. Taylor indulged in and observed her starry-eyed, hopeless romances through a fairy-tale lens.

Fearless has stood the test of time, as 14 years later it was featured on *Rolling Stone*'s 2022 list of the 100 Greatest Country Albums of All Time. Outside of the music industry, Taylor made history during her *Saturday Night Live* hosting debut, during which she became the first-ever celebrity host to write their own opening monologue as a fully-formed song.

What defines the era?

Fearless is not only an album littered with songs about love, heartbreak and hopeless romanticism. It was also the first time that we, as fans, were able to climb inside Taylor's imagination and live out generic teenage experiences through her fairy-tale vision.

And as for what *Fearless* became the catalyst for ... Taylor's sophomore album was her combining her country and pop princess personas, which would help position her solidly in two music genres. She had already made waves with her debut album, but *Fearless* truly propelled her into superstar territory.

What now defines the *Fearless* era, and what makes Taylor such a unique case study, is that while finding her feet as a musical icon, she also walked effortlessly in the shoes of a vulnerable 18-year-old gal. Fluctuating between writing about the trials and tribulations of young love, while simultaneously attending every prestigious awards show and showbiz event, Taylor managed to balance her heightened fame and glitz 'n' glam lifestyle with her 'regular girl' existence. Something that made her approachable, authentic and accessible to every other 18-year-old girl at the time.

Taylor's gal-pal era also started to emerge during this period. In 2008, she crossed paths with singer-songwriter Selena Gomez, who fans will know has been a significant and consistent figure in Taylor's life ever since. Taylor and Selena's relationship is one that fans have gushed over for years and one that probably established her as the ultimate girl's girl.

During an interview with *Seventeen* in October 2009, Selena was asked whether she had a specific friend she would turn to when it came to love and relationships. Selena – who was about 17 at the time – gave the sweetest answer: 'Every single problem I ever have is healable by Taylor Swift!' she shared. 'If I ever have an issue, Taylor has gone through it, because she's older than me, and she gives the most thought-out answers. And what I love about Taylor is that she does believe in the whole love story and Prince Charming and soulmates. Because of her, I haven't lost faith.'

Taylor herself, though, summed up *Fearless* in the best way possible on Twitter, back in 2021.

ALBUM STATS AND ACCOLADES

Fearless

Release Date:
11 November 2008
Debut on *Billboard* 200:
Number One, 11 weeks*
***Rolling Stone* Rating:** 4/5
Certified (RIAA):
One x Diamond

*non-consecutive

'*Fearless* was an album full of magic and curiosity, the bliss and devastation of youth. It was the diary of the adventures and explorations of a teenage girl who was learning tiny lessons with every new crack in the facade of the fairy-tale ending she'd been shown in the movies.'

Fearless outfit inspiration

Having achieved headliner status, it was no surprise that during her *Fearless* days, Taylor started exploring her style and embracing her individuality more. She was also 18 and so of course she was going to be experimenting further with fashion. So, if it's this era you're going for style-wise, you're definitely going to want to step it up a notch following her debut. Here's how:

SPARKLY AND GLITZY DRESSES – fringe is *highly* encouraged.

MINIDRESSES

PRINCESS GOWNS – the more medieval/period-looking, the better. Oh, and lots of velvet for this look is advised.

THE COWBOY BOOTS ARE STILL IN BUT HEELS HAVE ALSO MADE AN ENTRANCE

BIG, BOUNCY CURLS

FROSTED BLUE EYESHADOW

Other miscellaneous items:

THE NUMBER 13 PAINTED ON YOUR HAND – if you didn't already know, 13 is Taylor's lucky number and during her *Fearless* era, she displayed it noticeably on her hand during performances. She revealed the relevance of the number during a 2009 MTV interview, sharing:

'I was born on the 13th, I turned 13 on Friday the 13th, my first album went gold in 13 weeks. Also, my first song that ever went to Number One, it had a 13-second intro – I didn't even do that on purpose!'

Fearless is a really fun look to experiment with because there are a couple of ways you can go about it. First, let's unpack the medieval, velvet option that Taylor so famously wore during her *Fearless Tour*. Yes, you might be thinking, 'Where on earth am I going to find a dress with such specific requirements?' but I have a couple of options for you ...

Charity shops are a treasure trove when it comes to putting these outfits together and a great way to play dress-up while staying environmentally conscious. You just need to pop into every charity shop you see (an easy homework assignment for all you thrifters out there) and keep an eye out and you're sure to find the right look. Failing that, vintage stores and websites are goldmines for velvet medieval-esque fits. Because the dress will do all the talking, you won't need any jewellery – just style yourself some of those soft, bouncy curls and you're good to go.

Minidress *Fearless* Taylor is also quite self-explanatory but a lot easier to access. For this era, lots of sparkly silver and gold is a must-have – think Twenties flapper-style but more fitted and with the hems much shorter. Again, a lack of jewellery is advised to let the piece – quite literally – shine. Shoe-wise, a pair of knee-high black patent boots will do the trick, or even a pair of sparkly silver/gold ones to match.

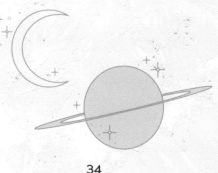

3.

SPEAK NOW

(2010)

Next up, *Speak Now*. Let's unpack the 2010 era, which feels like it was inspired by the first transition stage from adolescence into almost-adulthood.

First, though, it's important to comment on Taylor's writing credits for this album. While her previous album *Fearless* included seven songs penned solely by her, *Speak Now* broke that record. Rather than seek the help of some of the top songwriters in the business, Taylor authored EVERY. SINGLE. SONG. on the album herself.

Taylor has since spoken out about this decision and in the years following *Speak Now*'s release has shared how adamant she was to prove those who ever doubted her wrong.

'When I was 18, they were like, "She doesn't really write those songs." So my third album I wrote by myself as a reaction to that,' she told *Rolling Stone* in 2019.

Taylor has said that each song acts as a diary entry about the emotions she felt between the ages of 18 and 20. She spilled out the words she could never say – or regretted not saying to others – onto the pages of her music journal.

In the liner notes accompanying the album, Taylor expressed this by writing:

'These songs are made up of words I didn't say when the moment was right in front of me. These songs are open letters. Each is written with a specific person in mind, telling them what I meant to tell them in person.'

She also revealed why she settled on the album name *Speak Now*, while talking to *New York Magazine* in 2010. According to Taylor, the words – which she described as a metaphor – captured the essence of the album.

'That moment where it's almost too late, and you've got to either say what it is you are feeling or deal with the consequences forever,' she recalled. Taylor added that her third studio album seemed like the perfect opportunity for her to 'speak now or forever hold my peace', which is a direct reference from the record's title track.

A sense of growth can be seen in the myriad layers of *Speak Now*. Taylor adopts a more confessional, direct outlook, and although her fairy-tale references remain, her lyricism is undoubtedly more mature. Also, her willingness to experiment spilled into the album's production. Rather than being strictly country (Taylor had definitely not neglected her roots entirely), or just having hints of pop , *Speak Now* incorporates elements of power pop and pop rock. These developments can be heard in 'Better Than Revenge', 'The Story of Us' and 'Haunted'.

Taylor's third album went on to scoop her a new set of accolades and titles. At the 54th Grammy Awards in 2012, *Speak Now* was nominated for Best Country Album, while the single 'Mean' landed Best Country Song and Best Country Solo Performance.

It also became the first album since American rapper Lil Wayne's 2008 album *Tha Carter III* to sell over a million copies during its first week of release and debut at Number One on the *Billboard* 200. Not to mention bagging a Guinness World Record in 2010 for being the fastest-selling album in the US by a female country artist.

Plus, the *New York Times* was quick to dub Taylor as an artist now worthy of the megastardom title. It detailed that, in 2010, the music industry saw album sales 'plunge by more than 50 percent in the last decade'. Citing music downloading platforms as being responsible for the shift, they said that despite this, *Speak Now* sales proved that Taylor had 'transcended the limitations of genre' and had 'become a pop megastar'.

Then, at the end of 2011, Taylor was chosen as *Billboard* Women in Music's Woman of the Year. The award celebrates the most talented, influential and powerful women in the music industry, with *Billboard*'s former editorial director, Bill Werde, labelling her as 'an incredible role model'.

Upon Taylor winning the award, Werde made a significant commentary and observation of her character, which further backed up her commitment to the cause. He said: 'Taylor has shown the power of good songwriting with music that has transcended genres, and we're thrilled to recognise all of her successes over the past year by honouring her with the "*Billboard* Woman of the Year Award".

'At the young age of 21, Taylor has already made a major impact on music and has been an incredible role model for aspiring singers/songwriters and young women everywhere. I look forward to watching her career continue to flourish in the years to come.'

Most recently, Taylor has reminisced about *Speak Now*, sharing why the record means so much to her all these years on. While chatting on Instagram about *Taylor's Version* (a term which refers to her re-recordings), which she released on 2 December 2022, she said:

'I love this album because it tells a tale of growing up, flailing, flying and crashing ... and living to speak about it.'

What defines the era?

In one word, empowerment. Whether that is due to the fact that Taylor had three albums under her belt (and probably a newfound self-confidence/assurance that comes with more Grammy wins, world records and huge success) or simply that she was evolving into a more mature adult, *Speak Now* was an obvious move from the young girl-next-door vibe to a grown-up album.

From her confessional lyricism, her completely self-penned album and the obvious notion that Taylor was reflecting on her own growth, *Speak Now* can also be experienced as her last era as a fledgling adult.

Speak Now was also a time when Taylor was particularly conscious of her role-model persona. She'd always understood this importance, but crossing the line between teenager and 'official' adult came with added pressure to ensure that she was making the right impression on her younger fans. She told CBS News in 2011 that she thinks about 'a million people when [she's] getting dressed in the morning'.

'That's just part of my life now. I think it's my responsibility to know it, and to be conscious of it. And it would be really easy to say, "You know, I'm 21 now. I do what I want. You raise your kids." But that's not the truth of it,' she added. 'The truth of it is that every singer out there with songs on the radio is raising the next generation so make your words count.'

Speak Now has become one of the most renowned albums in country pop music history. Having already stood the test of time over a decade later, it's quite clear that it's a culturally important piece of art. Thanks to its skilful songwriting, emotive themes and Taylor's courage to wear her heart on her sleeve, the whole era is dripping with relatability whatever age you are.

Speak Now outfit inspiration

If you've become a lifelong Swiftie because of this album, chances are you're going to want to attend the *Eras Tour* looking like a walking, talking version of *Speak Now*.

I LOVE this era for its adaptability because you can either rock up to your chosen arena in a preppy wardrobe circa 2010, or you can create your own elaborate version of the *Speak Now World Tour*. Or, if you're feeling like you want to collide both era styles, what's stopping you?

Let's deconstruct the first option. When not performing, Taylor's casual style choices were very cutesy and country clubby. During this time, she would dress in cable-knit sweaters, collared dresses and frilled blouses paired with oxford heels or knee-high boots. In even more casual circumstances, flannel shirts, a leather satchel and an oversized knitted beanie sufficed. Just make sure that your bangs are curled and styled in a side parting, while the rest of your hair is tucked neatly into the oh-so-2010 hat.

If you think about it, this is such an autumn girlie look, so Swifties with a penchant for oversized jumpers, pleated skirts and patterned tights, you'll already be set. However, if your idea of *Speak Now* get-up is fitting with the colour scheme of the era, plus Taylor's magnificent stadium tour aesthetic, firstly, it's ALL about the colour purple. Wardrobe-wise, there was still an inkling of fairy-tale Taylor who was not quite done with her whimsical style.

So, for stage-ready Taylor, there's a huge focus on the tulle dresses and, honestly, the more over-the-top and prom-like the better. This *Speak Now* dress-up can include a version of the cute halter-neck Fifties-style purple dress Taylor wore when she invited Selena Gomez on stage during her Madison Square Garden show.

Now is also a good time to point out that, alongside mixing and matching your perfect *Speak Now* fit, you'll want to get practising your hand hearts. Back in 2011, the *New York Times* christened Taylor as the 'Queen of Hand Hearts' after the action became a staple part of her performative practice during the *Speak Now World Tour*.

During a chat with the newspaper, Taylor explained that the symbol means, 'something between "I love you" and "thank you"'. She described it as a 'sweet, simple' message that she could deliver to her fans, 'without saying a word'. For the ultimate Instagram photo composition, you can make the sign with your hands above your head – as was customary during her live show – or put your hand heart to your chest. Alternatively, position it in front of your eyes and give your sweetest smile.

While I'm peppering in the fun extra references from the era, don't forget to write your favourite lyrics from the album in Sharpie down the side of your left arm. Taylor started doing this while she was on the road touring the album and over the course of the year-long *Speak Now World Tour*, penned around 81 lyrics from both her own songs and those of other artists.

Only the lyrics most meaningful to Taylor made it onto her arm, but for the fans, it also felt like a personal invitation into Taylor's Spotify playlist. Taylor's collection of powerful song lyrics made it feel like she had a support system made up of some of the most influential musicians both past and present up on stage with her every night. Of course, because this is a Get Ready With Me for the *Eras Tour Speak Now* style, it would make sense to pick lines from the album.

Oh, and one more thing: wherever you can, figure out a way to incorporate a koi fish into your outfit, whether it be a temporary tattoo, a piece of jewellery featuring the fish or a creative eye-make-up look (yellow sparkly gems would be ace here).

Avid Swifties will know that koi fish are historically important to Taylor, as she had four printed on her blue *Speak Now* era guitar. This is the guitar Taylor strummed on during the emotional acoustic section of the show while wearing *that* purple chiffon dress.

Just for an extra bit of Taylor trivia, the blue koi fish guitar made a reappearance during two of her *Midnights* music videos: 'Lavender Haze' and 'Anti-Hero'. The 'Anti-Hero' video was released on 21 October 2022 along with the whole of *Midnights*, while 'Lavender Haze' followed in January 2023. Swiftie theorists surmised that the *Speak Now*-era koi fish was a hint that *Taylor's Version* of the album was just around the corner.

Whether a coincidence or not, Taylor eventually released the re-recorded version of *Speak Now* in December 2023. If you ask me, not only does she have one of the most genius marketing brains on the planet, but she's also pretty damn good at keeping secrets. Just imagine having to drip-feed such symbolic clues for almost a year and not be able to shout from the rooftops how excited you are for what's to come.

Anyway, koi fish conspiracies aside, I feel like I've pretty much got this style down to a T.

PREPPY CASUAL ATTIRE – anything knitted.

TULLE, TULLE AND MORE TULLE – whether you opt for a dress like the one on the album cover or create your own version of stage Taylor, just make sure that whatever you pick is purple! FYI just type 'tulle dress' into Google and voilà, you'll be greeted with corset cami styles, homecoming vibes, bridesmaid-esque fits and tiered maxidresses. You can also opt for a layered tulle skirt and pair it with a top of your choice – it's up to you!

BOUNCY, FLOWING HAIR – the curls are still a major statement element of *Speak Now*.

RED LIPSTICK IS A MUST

FALSE EYELASHES AND THE ODD BIT OF WINGED EYELINER – remember, Taylor was getting a little older so experimenting with more mature make-up looks.

Other miscellaneous items:

LYRIC BOOK – to pluck your favourite *Speak Now* line from.

SHARPIE – to write said line on your left arm.

REMEMBER TO MASTER THE ART OF THE HAND HEART

KOI FISH ACCESSORIES

If you're looking to add some themed fun into your next Taylor event for you and your friends, make the below drink to fit into the *Speak Now* era! Recipes have been peppered through the book so you can pick your favourite era and make your event as thematic as possible.

THE LAST KISS

INGREDIENTS

Crushed ice
75ml freshly squeezed lemon juice
50ml fresh orange juice
50ml pineapple juice
25ml grenadine
Ginger ale or ginger beer
Pineapple and/or orange slices, to garnish

METHOD

* Fill a cocktail shaker two-thirds full with crushed ice and all three juices.

* Shake well.

* Strain into a tall glass filled with crushed ice.

* Top with the grenadine and some ginger ale or ginger beer.

* Stir gently.

* Serve garnished with slices of pineapple and/or orange.

4.

RED
(2012)

Meet Taylor 4.0. From an aesthetics perspective, purple was out and red was in, but let me tell you, this simple colour shift was only the beginning of Taylor spreading her wings. Taylor herself told *Rolling Stone* in 2020 that the *Red* album was 'the beginning of everything that I'm doing now'.

On recollection, *Red* also marked Taylor's acceptance as an artist into the larger world of music. It was a time when fans who only viewed her music as a guilty pleasure decided it was actually cool to like and listen to Taylor Swift and shout it from the rooftops rather than hide behind their headphones.

Whether Taylor now being 'cool' should be cited as a turning point is debatable, but it does affirm that there had been a major shift in public opinion, even though the critics had more or less always been on her side, championing her from the sidelines.

This surge of new fans was due to *Red* being way more experimental in terms of genre. Specific tracks like 'Red', 'Treacherous', 'Begin Again' and 'I Almost Do' still retained a country edge, due to their classic acoustic openings, recognisable vocal harmonies, and that all-important slide guitar. It meant that, even though Taylor was pushing her musical future in a more 'commercial' direction, it still allowed her to stick to her first love *and* be entered into award categories of multiple genres.

When genre-bending, Taylor enlisted the help of a bunch of new producers, writers and musicians to help her transition into a different sonic landscape. These included Swedish pop legend Max Martin, who is behind some of the biggest hits *ever*, from Britney Spears's '... Baby One More Time' to Katy Perry's 'I Kissed a Girl'. Not to mention Shellback (Karl Johan Schuster), whose discography also includes Britney, Ariana Grande, Avril Lavigne, Adele and Maroon 5, and Jeff Bhasker, who produced Harry Styles's self-titled album.

Other notable collaborators at this time include Dann Huff, Dan Wilson, Jacknife Lee and Butch Walker. Taylor still stuck by her long-time collaborator Nathan Chapman for this album, but it would be her penultimate record working with him. She also called upon the musical knowledge of Ed Sheeran and Snow Patrol's Gary Lightbody during sessions for *Red*, who again helped her edge away from the consistent country sounds of her three earliest records. While Sheeran performed on the much-loved track 'Everything Has Changed', Lightbody offered his pop ballad expertise on 'The Last Time'.

Taylor musically reinvented herself on *Red*, all the while, though, she stuck to her guns and held on tightly to her secret weapon: her undeniable storytelling talent, which had allowed her to resonate with millions of people around the world for the last six years. This can be heard 'all too well' in that exact track.

According to the history books, Taylor formed the track during the *Speak Now World Tour* rehearsals. As the story goes, she presented almost 10 minutes' worth of lyrics to her bandmates before working with co-writer Liz Rose to form the song.

Linking to the 'track five theory', which is where fans have noticed that the fifth song on Taylor's albums is usually a particularly personal and vulnerable song to her, 'All Too Well' is arguably the most famous of all. Taylor later explained during an Instagram Live that she didn't realise she was doing it, but as she was making the albums perhaps she was subconsciously 'putting a very vulnerable, personal, honest, emotional song as track five'. She explains it's something she does with purpose now that her fans have pointed it out.

Some may say 'All Too Well' was the first time she put such sincerity, depth and sadness into a song about breaking up with someone. Whether it was because it was her longest song on the album or because Taylor detailed every sad, mundane and ordinary scenario, the narrative was thoroughly agonising.

While Taylor hasn't to date spoken publicly about the relationship that inspired the album, it's widely thought that *Red* was born from the heartbreak she endured following the split. According to Taylor, it's a 'metaphor for how messy a real break-up is' and even shared that the 'mystery' ex contacted her after listening to the tracks and described them as 'bittersweet'. After listening to *Red* again with an analytical brain, and trying to tap into the emotions felt by Taylor at the time, it's easy to hear how she's captured such visceral, raw pain that branches from a break-up. Each song was clearly born from the emotional destruction a person experiences in the aftermath of a split – Taylor even recalled to *Rolling Stone* in 2020 that she was doing 'a lot of vacillation and changing' during that period.

Taylor's frankness about the album has been identified many times. From the range of 'intense love, intense frustration, jealousy and confusion' acting as the catalysts for the tracks, she has also said retrospectively that she felt 'nothing in between'. Being so emotionally overwhelmed by her situation led to her sharing: 'There's nothing beige about any of those feelings.'

And when dropping *Red (Taylor's Version)* in 2021, Taylor said in an Instagram post:

'Musically and lyrically, *Red* resembled a heartbroken person. It was all over the place, a fractured mosaic of feelings that somehow all fit together at the end.'

Yes, the concept of heartbreak-inspiring music is nothing new, but there's something about *Red* that feels so intense and poignant that it's hard to compare it to any other record dealing with the same themes.

Red spent seven weeks atop the *Billboard* 200 in the US. This feat made Taylor the first female act and the second artist since The Beatles to achieve three consecutive albums that each spent *at least* six weeks at the top spot. Aside from this, the Recording Industry Association of America (RIAA) certified the album Platinum a cool seven times.

Grammy-wise, it was nominated for four, including Album of the Year, Best Country Album, Best Country Song and Best Country Duo/Group Performance. Taylor also bagged two nominations for the former award at the 2013 Country Music Association Awards and the 2014 Academy of Country Music Awards. While she didn't pick up a Grammy for *Red*, she did win the Top Album and Top Country Album at the 2013 *Billboard* Music Awards.

Funnily enough, that the album missed out on a Grammy really didn't make any difference to critics, who have gone on to assert that *Red* is in fact Taylor's best body of work. To *Clash*, *Red* demonstrated the turning point in Taylor's career, whereby it 'was the first time Taylor actively stepped away from the pretty dresses and southern girl chic' in order to discern the 'old-fashioned listeners'. They also said that it was 'both ground-breaking and wildly commercial' because Taylor 'opened a door for every other musician' that allowed them to transcend genres if they felt like it.

For Pitchfork, *Red*'s sonic leap meant Taylor was pushing her music to 'the highest aspirations of her songwriting'. They also commended her for breaking out from her comfort zone 'to stray into the interzone between pop and country'. And for Rob Sheffield of *Rolling Stone*, who said in 2021 that *Red* was where Taylor 'proved herself not just the supreme pop songwriter of her generation, but one of the all-timers', *Red* 'wasn't her first masterwork', but 'the one that established the Swiftian universe as a place where every lost scarf is a ticking time bomb that can take years to explode into a classic song'.

I love *Red* for all of its nuances, reinvention and distinctiveness from anything Taylor had done before. Also, for its batch of surprises, especially learning that, despite being the poppiest album she'd released at that point, Taylor took major influence from one of the most celebrated folk artists of all time: Joni Mitchell. Specifically, her 1971 album, *Blue*.

Even though the two albums are so different sonically, the vulnerability and honesty is where the similarities lie. 'She wrote it about her deepest pains and her most haunting demons,' Taylor reflected. 'Songs like "River", which is just about her regrets and doubts of herself – I think this album is my favourite because it explores somebody's soul so deeply.' And if there's one thing about Taylor, she's very much all for baring her soul, both for cathartic reasons and to help others who may be feeling the same way.

What defines the era?

Red is a hard one to sum up in just a few words. It's significant because it marks an obvious turning point in Taylor's career. It's a huge visual *and* sonic shift for Taylor. Her collaborations with poppier industry people helped her to step out of her comfort zone and broaden her appeal to a more diverse range of listeners without alienating her core fanbase. Despite running full speed down a path of world domination, Taylor still found a way to be relatable.

In contrast, to Taylor, *Red* was also a reaction to her questioning her relevancy. To her fans, it's hard to understand how someone like Taylor could ever question her own abilities. Surely, with a cabinet full of awards confirming your talent, the one thing you'd be sure of is yourself? But alas, this wasn't the case and part of what defines *Red* is Taylor's internal insecurities coupled with her determination and hunger to succeed.

When talking to *Rolling Stone* in 2020, she said: 'I've always been very aware of my own sort of relevancy and mortality. My career started when I was 16, so by 22, I was already on some days feeling like old news.' This internal struggle is widely recognised in her unreleased track 'Nothing New', which featured indie star Phoebe Bridgers and was released on *Red (Taylor's Version)* in 2021. The song was originally written in 2012 with the intention of making it on to the album the first time around and came to life when Taylor learned to play the Appalachian dulcimer. According to Taylor, it's inspired by Joni Mitchell's 'A Case of You' and wrestles with rhetorical questions about change. She openly talks about the struggles and challenges young female artists face in the music industry and confronts the hypocrisy and double standards that encourage them to be young, wild and free, but then judge them for being so when they get a little older. The track also alludes to a throwaway society that values young and shiny things, but one that soon loses interest once your novelty wears off.

Taylor opened up about watching 'newer, cooler' artists emerge onto the scene almost continuously, which made her rethink her current strategy as a musician. Yes, she loved country music. Yes, she had always stood by her earlier material. And yes, she was *never* disheartened by it. But the said surge in new talent did make her think that *Red* was the time she needed to innovate, explore and evolve who she was as an artist.

Taylor eventually described the process as an 'interesting wrestling match' with her 'own fears of remaining stagnant that made *Red* the joy ride that it ended up being'. And if we're talking about the actual colour red, it symbolises powerful and unstable passion, which is a clear and recurring theme throughout Taylor's fourth studio album.

She became the first solo artist in two decades to headline a stadium tour in Australia – the last had been Madonna with her 1993 *The Girlie Show*. During her *Red World Tour*, Taylor was also the first female artist in history to sell out the Sydney Football Stadium. Oh, and it became the highest-grossing tour from a country artist in history at that time. It brought Taylor a staggering $150 million, surpassing her icons Tim McGraw and Faith Hill's Soul2Soul II co-headline tour.

Red was an era with a lot of firsts.

Red outfit inspiration

Despite the *Red* album being such a mixed bag musically, Taylor's aesthetic remained consistent – 2012 Taylor was in a league of her own and this can be visually identified in an instant.

ALBUM STATS AND ACCOLADES
Red
Release Date:
2 October 2012
Debut on *Billboard* 200:
Number One, seven weeks
***Rolling Stone* Rating:**
3.5/5
Certified (RIAA):
Seven x Platinum

The first drastic difference was her hair. For so long, fans had been used to Taylor's huge, bouncy country-girl curls and their honey-blonde shade. Alongside trialling a more 'grown-up' shade, the most obvious change was that the curls had gone. Whether it was a conscious effort to appear more sophisticated, or Taylor simply fancied something different, her straight tresses gave her a striking edge compared to her previous wild and unruly head of hair.

But 2012 was also the year of the fringe and Taylor jumped on the trend during her *Red* period, and of course, beyond. She's seldom seen without a fringe these days and it's become a trademark part of her adult-era look.

On to the second drastic difference: the colour red threading the era together. Now we all know Taylor and her insistence on the details – her perfectionist nature is part of why we love her. It shows she cares and is passionate about her craft, but also that when she has a vision, it's paramount that it comes to life.

When it comes to the colour red, it's dispersed through almost every element of the album. From Taylor's mic stands during the world tour, the outfits of her back-up dancers, the smoke machines and spotlights, and even her collection of guitars.

Besides the colour neatly sewing everything together, Taylor's *Red* era also proved to be the perfect time for her to display her love of all things vintage. Her take on Fifties fashion was particularly evident here. Be it the pin-up red lip (which then became her staple) or her winged eyeliner, Taylor's inclusion of the iconic Rockabilly high-waisted shorts was another statement *Red* element. Those who were experimenting with fashion during their early to late teenage years at this time will specifically remember the sailor-style shorts with the six big gold buttons on the front.

Of course, Taylor didn't slip on Fifties ensembles straight from the vaults, she jazzed them up a bit to give them more of a twenty-first-century zest and to infuse an element of her own personal style.

If you study some of Taylor's stage outfits at this time, the black shorts were a constant. Whether they were paired with a sparkly red fitted mesh top, worn with a lace cream Peter Pan collared piece, or a sheer white blouse with a statement collar and sleeves to the elbow, the style and fit never changed. Taylor even conjured up her own sequined bodysuit that mirrored the design. If you're comfortable wearing such items, her ombré black-and-red offering is a definite showstopping *Eras Tour* ensemble.

Taylor's *Red* vintage fits weren't just tight-fitting and strictly stage-worthy, though. Oversized white T-shirts with statement messages on the front were also on-brand and whenever she wore them on-stage, they were always accompanied by a black bowler hat.

Take your pick from some of the most famous offerings, the first taking inspiration from one of her tracks: 'We are never getting back together like ever'. Or how about the ever-famous 'Not a lot going on at the moment'. Alternatively, you can go for the tongue-in-cheek 'Who's Taylor Swift anyway? Ew', which demonstrates her ability to poke fun at herself.

I've not forgotten you autumn girls, by the way. In among Taylor's ever-present sequins, Fifties-inspired fits and the ultimate stage glam that *Red* served, the then 22-year-old didn't neglect her beloved fall attire. So, if you're not one for purchasing one-off outfits that will be shoved to the back of your closet post the Eras concert, or you're more comfortable in Taylor's casual wardrobe, I've got you. Let's face it, a black-and-red sequinned bodysuit may look *fire*, but it's not really a sustainable option if you're only planning on wearing it once. Instead, let's dip into Taylor's collection of knit scarves, saddle-bag purses and raincoats. Plus, her array of nautical T-shirts that are just as synonymous with the *Red* era.

When looking at the latter, Taylor switched back and forth between navy blue and white tops, and black and red. She paired them with red pleated skirts, skinny jeans and Capri pants, while sometimes accessorising with her trusty bowler hat. Other memorable moments from Taylor's street-style *Red* era include vintage-looking polka-dot dresses, navy-and-white varsity jackets, Vans/Converse-style trainers, or sweet brogues.

My last piece of advice? If you're struggling with any of the quintessentially *Red* pieces, it doesn't matter so long as you rock up to the show in something red. Let's round up the most essential *Red* pieces once more:

STRAIGHTEN! THOSE! CURLS!

INCORPORATE THE COLOUR RED *SOMEWHERE*

A LOOSE FIFTIES INFLUENCE WITH A TWENTY-FIRST-CENTURY EDGE – high-waisted shorts are crucial here.

Anybody notice the absence of cowboy boots? For casual Taylor, it's all about BROGUES AND FASHION 'SNEAKERS'.

RED LIPS, WINGED EYELINER

PICK UP A BOWLER HAT

SEQUINS, SEQUINS AND MORE SEQUINS

OVERSIZED STATEMENT T-SHIRTS

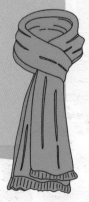

T-SHIRT PAINTING MASTERCLASS

One of Taylor's most iconic outfits when singing from the *Red* album has her wearing slogan tees with different phrases with either quotes from her songs, or her now iconic 'not a lot going on at the moment' line. If you're up for some DIY, you can create your own at home and here's how ...

Things you'll need

♥ Some newspaper or an old sheet to drape over the work surface so that you don't get paint everywhere

♥ A freshly ironed white T-shirt (or plural, depending on whether you want to recreate all of them) in your size

♥ Art pencil and paper (optional)

♥ A fine paintbrush

♥ Some red and black fabric paint

How to make them

♥ First, decide which phrase you'll be painting onto your T-shirt. From 'We are never getting back together like ever', 'Not a lot going on at the moment' to 'Who's Taylor Swift anyway? Ew', this craft is totally up there for all *Red*-era Swifties. Of course, you don't have to use these phrases either – you can transfer the idea to any era and paint on the Taylor lyrics that resonate with you the most.

♥ Cover your workstation with some newspaper or an old sheet and lay out your T-shirt as tight as you can. Ideally, you don't want any creases or folds.

♥ If you're copying the exact Taylor designs, paint the words onto the T-shirt in the same colour and style. Sometimes it helps to draw the design onto a piece of paper or even the shirt first with an art pencil so that you have some sort of reference, rather than jumping in freehand.

♥ Leave the T-shirts to dry according to the directions on the paint before moving/wearing them.

Extra tip: If art isn't your forté but you still want to get involved in this craft, not to worry. Just order some stencils to give you a helping hand, but make sure that they're of the right size to cover a T-shirt. And if you can, see if you can get one in the font 'Tungsten Semibold' as it's the one Taylor used for the look.

5.

1989
(2014)

The year of the GIRL SQUAD. We know Taylor has always flown the flag for the gals, from offering us a metaphorical shoulder to cry on, to promoting self-love and body positivity, and being the fearless female empowerment warrior that she is. But 1989 was the era when she physically assembled *her* tribe.

From 2013 to 2016, Taylor's pals began generating plenty of media attention when they were regularly photographed hanging out together. The 'squad' consisted of her BFF Selena Gomez, plus a selection of equally strong and powerful women, including Karlie Kloss, Gigi Hadid, Martha Hunt, Jaime King, Cara Delevingne and Lena Dunham. To mention a few …

Taylor's squad already had their own achievements and fan base, and they were just as empowering by themselves as they were as a collective. However, their safety in numbers gave them the *ultimate* power. Isn't that what friendship is about? Reciprocating love, support and standing up for one another when it counts the most?

This loyalty and support was demonstrated at its best in the 'Bad Blood' music video. Starring Lily Aldridge, Zendaya, Hayley Williams, Gigi Hadid, Ellie Goulding, Hailee Steinfeld, Lena Dunham, Karlie Kloss, Serayah, Jessica Alba, Martha Hunt, Ellen Pompeo, Mariska Hargitay, Cara Delevingne and Cindy Crawford, the video referenced one of Taylor's friends betraying her, only for her 'squad' to come out in full force and take revenge.

Aside from having Taylor's back in the superhero/sci-fi music video, the squad members have publicly shown their support and solidarity for the star in real life. When touring the world with the album in 2015, Taylor brought out Karlie Kloss, Martha Hunt, Gigi Hadid, Kendall Jenner, Serena Williams and Cara Delevingne to the London stage, where they walked the runway during her live rendition of 'Style'.

Back in the US, Taylor had not one date to the 2015 MTV Video Music Awards, but nine. Taking over the red carpet, she and some of her 'Bad Blood' crew epitomised girl power as they all celebrated her big win: Video of the Year.

One of Taylor's most significant friendships musically during *1989* was with the producer Jack Antonoff. After first meeting at the MTV European Music Awards in November 2012, the pair would begin a now-celebrated musical partnership just one year later. Their musical forces joined for the first time when they co-wrote and co-produced the soundtrack 'Sweeter Than Fiction' for British film *One Chance*. Many critics say this laid the foundations for their ground-breaking work on *1989*.

Jack helped to produce a number of songs on *1989*, including 'Out of the Woods', 'I Wish You Would' and the deluxe edition bonus track, 'You Are In Love'. Following the album's 2014 release, Jack shared a still image of the duo's track, 'Out of the Woods', alongside a heartfelt caption documenting his love for their working relationship.

'Will one day write an essay on the different production I used on the song + how much working with Taylor on it has meant to me. She's a wonderful artist,' he enthused.

The significance of these friendships is something Taylor recalls to *ELLE* in 2019: 'Something about "we're in our young twenties!" hurls people together into groups that can feel like your chosen family ... And maybe they will be for the rest of your life. Or maybe they'll just be your comrades for an important phase, but not forever. It's sad but sometimes when you grow, you outgrow relationships. You may leave behind friendships along the way, but you'll always keep the memories.'

Your young twenties are often about new beginnings, and for

Taylor, the beginnings of her new life in New York was something she wanted to celebrate in this album, too. Taylor opened the album with a mission statement, declaring that New York had been waiting for her. Not only did it symbolise her love of her new life in the chic Tribeca neighbourhood, but it also highlighted her sense of newfound freedom. The Big Apple welcomed her with open arms and she fell head over heels into its chaos and magic.

Leaving her roots behind physically also allowed for an uprooting musically. Inspired by New York's diverse music scene, this era saw Taylor doff her cap to the decade of her birth by experimenting with sounds of Eighties-inspired synthpop. Annie Lennox and Peter Gabriel were two of the main influences behind the album. To Taylor, it was Lennox's 'intense' thoughts, lyrically and sonically, that she drew influence from and Gabriel's distinct synth-pop sound that 'created an atmosphere behind what he was singing, rather than a produced track'.

Taylor also shed the heartbroken persona she had carried for many years and came out the other side thriving and ready to celebrate. 'Welcome to New York' and 'Clean' open and close the album with an overall motif of self-discovery.

During the making of 1989, Taylor understood that trying something new was non-negotiable for her career-wise. She told PopCrush: 'I don't have the option of making music that sounds just like what I've done before.

'People will see right through it. They'll see that I was lazy,' she recalled, while adding that her label also begged her to include three country-esque tracks.

'At a certain point, if you chase two rabbits, you lose them both,' she concluded.

1989 gave Taylor many accolades, too. It stands out as her

bestselling album, having sold more than 15 million copies to date. It gave Taylor seven Grammy nominations, for which she won three: Best Pop Vocal Album, Best Music Video for 'Bad Blood' and Album of the Year, which she accepted alongside her pal and collaborator, Jack Antonoff. *1989* was Taylor's second time winning the award, which made her the first female artist to claim it twice.

Continuing on the triumph train, the album shifted over 1 million copies in its first week, which according to Nielsen SoundScan was the biggest seven-day sales of a release since 2002. Taylor set yet another world record: becoming the first artist to hit the 1 million sales in a week milestone three times.

Alongside this, Taylor scooped her second *Billboard* Woman of the Year award, partly thanks to the album's success and partly thanks to her *1989* era's flourishing feminist consciousness.

What's incredible about *1989*'s album sales is that Taylor and her label, Big Machine Records, pulled the record from free streaming services, most notably Spotify. It sparked a widespread discourse among the industry, especially in terms of streaming and compensation for artists.

During Taylor's *Billboard* Woman of the Year cover story, Scott Borchetta, CEO of Big Machine (and the man who signed her, way back in 2005), admitted that his hopes weren't initially sky-high for the album sales, purely due to the fact that the music business climate at that time was being threatened by free streaming sites.

Borchetta said: 'When you have the entire industry saying, "Well, it might only be 800,000, but that's a great number," you start to question if the market could bear it.

'My job is to make sure [Taylor] had all the information.'

Of course, he had 'learned a long time ago: Don't ever doubt the power of Taylor Swift'.

What defines the album?

'I was born in 1989, reinvented for the first time in 2014,' Taylor shared in a handwritten note on Instagram the day she released *Taylor's Version*. Around the time of the release in 2014, she told *Billboard* that she regards *1989* as her 'starting over'. Fans and critics alike may have said that *Red* was when Taylor's career really took off in a different trajectory, but *1989* was when she truly stepped into her pop shoes and embraced her rebirth.

The album is contradictory in the best possible ways. Drawing colossal influence from the glossy synth sounds of the Eighties, it is nostalgic, musically and thematically. Taylor had emerged from the pits of *Red*'s heartbreak and was alive and kicking to tell her story – to divulge her emotions and reflections now that she was on the other side of it. She was now hopeful for the future, for what New York could offer and for what was around the corner for 24-year-old Taylor.

1989 is all about overcoming something devastating and creating something beautiful out of it. You could also say that *1989* was the era that proved Taylor's marketing savviness tenfold. In April 2014, she announced a livestream at the top of New York's Empire State Building. A selected crowd of lucky fans were treated to a once-in-a-lifetime performance of the album's first single, 'Shake It Off', which was followed by a full-blown promotional press tour. You couldn't watch TV, buy a magazine or scroll on social media without seeing Taylor's face.

The *1989* album was a turning point for Swifties and their relationship with Taylor, too. A string of mega fans were able to meet their hero when Taylor publicly invited them to her house on television during the press tour.

The year 2014 was also when she began putting on her

Secret Sessions, the fan-only listening parties where Taylor would preview her new albums for a select number of lucky Swifties. Fans – specifically selected by Taylor – would get an invite via a DM, phone call or email from her fan club, Taylor Nation, asking them to one of her homes for a sneak peek of the unreleased songs. Therefore giving them the ultimate Taylor Swift experience. This was a huge deal for them and for Taylor, as it represented their reciprocal give-and-take relationship.

Such elaborate marketing strategies, combined with Taylor's all-important personal touch and allegiance to her fans, turned *1989* into a cultural moment. A pop manifesto that aimed – and succeeded – in proving the criticism wrong, personally and artistically. All laced together with an overwhelming sense of taking back one's identity with a glittering of girl power.

1989 outfit inspiration

If you're rocking up as *1989* Taylor to the *Eras* concert, may I first suggest that you do so with your best gal pals on each arm? Complete with a Polaroid to capture this wholesome moment.

As well as *really* changing up her sound during this era, Taylor also opted for a monumental style transformation. Of course, the bangs stayed put, but she bravely swept them into the thick, full side parting that few can get away with. The side bangs were also accompanied by Taylor's unforgettably fabulous short bob.

Let's take a look at some of the essential wardrobe items that reflect the *1989* era:

CROP TOPS AND SKATER SKIRTS – these can be casual or stage-ready.

SHORT SHORTS – Taylor began showing off her never-ending pins during the *1989* years.

MATCHING TWO-PIECE SETS – think clean lines and laid-back design elements, as casual Taylor was more subdued.

COLOUR BLOCKING IS ESSENTIAL – Taylor's 2016 Grammy look is a great example of what I mean here. For the ceremony, she donned an orange bandeau paired with a fuchsia pink maxiskirt.

SPARSE (OR ZERO) ACCESSORIES – the focus was on the clean-line cut of clothing.

WORLD TOUR TAYLOR STEPPED THINGS UP A NOTCH IN TERMS OF THE EDGINESS – while NYC Taylor was cool, calm and collected and ever the chic millennial, she consulted her sequin dealer to come up with some show-stopping bustiers and jumpsuits.

DON'T FORGET THOSE ALL-IMPORTANT PALE-PINK OR BLACK-FRAMED SUNGLASSES

DON'T! FORGET! YOUR! POLAROID!

Starting with casual Taylor, first, I recommend you close your eyes and picture yourself living your best life in New York City. Your days consist of lunching with friends, strutting the famous streets with an iced coffee in hand and hitting up all the best high-end stores for said twin sets. If that sounds like you, you probably need to own a white co-ord set consisting of a fitted shift miniskirt and a matching top. Let me say that it doesn't need to be white, nor does it have to be fitted. A two-piece shirt and skirt set is really all you need so long as there's no detailing or patterns, and it remains one colour. Minimalism is key here.

When it comes to colour blocking, you can do it in any way that makes you feel the most comfortable, be it an exact replica of Taylor's Grammy's fit, or some high-waisted, pleated, wide-leg trousers in pink coupled with an oversize orange shirt. As long as you go all out on the colour blocking, it'll be obvious you're channelling Taylor. Again, Show Taylor requires plenty of sequins, jumpsuits and twin sets with an edgier twist. A look that comes up time and time again in this era is the metallic blue and purple skater skirts that she paired with sparkly bomber jackets. Easy enough to replicate with some of your favourite high-street brands or plenty of independent sellers, Glittergal Taylor is a really fun look to portray.

6.

reputation
(2017)

The 'America's musical sweetheart' persona that Taylor had worked so hard to sculpt over the years was instantly (yet temporarily) buried upon the release of *reputation* in 2017.

reputation ushered in Taylor's villain era slicker than her hair on the album's front cover. Her 'don't mess with me' attitude was partly embraced by the negative public scrutiny and bad press she faced, mostly resulting from the now-infamous feud with Kanye West and Kim Kardashian. It says something about an artist's character when they rise from a particularly bad spot – i.e. being dubbed a 'snake' – dust themselves off and walk away with their head held high. *And* a pocket full of cash generated from leaning into the version of herself that the media had created. But Taylor didn't need to give her side of the story or feed the hungry press, she simply needed to drop a newspaper-motif album cover that depicted the relentless tabloid coverage.

'Yeah, this is the character you created for me, let me just hide behind it,' she explained to *Vogue*.

Entering her edgiest and darkest era yet, no song defines the mood of the album better than the electropop 'Look What You Made Me Do'. The music video, which was a burn book (a term that originated from the 2004 film *Mean Girls*, referring to a book used for starting rumours, gossip or complaining about people), was filled with symbolic references to all the moments her character had been questioned or she'd received bad press. It was a satirical representation of her fallen reputation.

Ironically, *reputation*, which was also Taylor's last album under the Big Machine record label, was written when she had disappeared from the public gaze completely, amid intense scrutiny. During this era, aside from when she was scheduled to perform, Taylor retreated from her beloved awards ceremonies. It's a known fact that ever since her debut, she had been a familiar face at almost every event going, from the VMAs to the Grammys, so her absence was noted.

Taylor took this vanishing act and ran with it during the promotion of the album, when fans, the press and the music industry witnessed her marketing prowess once again. At noon on 18 August 2017 – three months before the release of *reputation* – the internet ground to a halt on the realisation that Taylor Swift had completely wiped her social media presence. Plus, she proceeded to unfollow EVERY. SINGLE. PERSON. she was following on Instagram.

Taylor's disappearance was her way of ensuring that *reputation* did all the talking. The references, symbolism and attention to detail littered throughout the album and its visual accompaniments were more than capable of getting her point across. It was also another example of the major shade Taylor was throwing during her *reputation* era.

'There will be no further explanation. There will just be reputation,' she dropped when breaking her social media silence.

Despite the overwhelming darkness of the era, Taylor didn't let the misanthropes rain on her parade. Songs like 'Gorgeous' and 'Delicate' chronicled the beginnings of what proved to be a long-term relationship. Taylor has since explained the journey she went on during the writing process for *reputation*. She described it as a linear timeline that started with how she felt when she began work on the album and progressed to her change of emotions upon completion. Additionally, when revealing that the album was inspired by the fantasy series *Game of Thrones*, Taylor shared that she split the lyrical breadth in two. The first leans into the downsides of fame and her anger towards the never-ending negative narratives, while the second documents how love will prevail, no matter how tumultuous other aspects of your life may be.

On the themes of the latter, Taylor described those early courting days as finding 'something sacred throughout all the battle cries'.

Taylor told *Entertainment Weekly* in 2019: 'These songs were half based on what I was going through, but seeing them through a *Game of Thrones* filter.

'"Look What You Made Me Do" is literally Arya Stark's kill list,' she shared, before adding that 'King of My Heart' was influenced by Khal Drogo and Daenerys.

'It's even got this post-hook of drums – I wanted them to sound like Dothraki drums,' Taylor noted.

And if you need any more convincing that Taylor is a major *GoT* fan, she confessed that she wrote a couple of the songs based on some of the Season 7 storylines.

'"I Did Something Bad" I wrote after Arya and Sansa conspire to kill Littlefinger. That and "Look What You Made Me Do" are very Cersei vibes, too. Daenerys as well,' she expressed.

ALBUM STATS AND ACCOLADES
reputation
Release Date:
10 November 2017
Debut on *Billboard* 200:
Number One, four weeks[*]
***Rolling Stone* Rating:** 4/5
Certified (RIAA):
Three x Platinum

*non-consecutive

Fantasy series aside, little did Taylor know that she would soon become close friends with one of the show's biggest stars, Sophie Turner.

Amid all the fighting talk, one must take a moment to acknowledge the achievements of Taylor's self-penned love-and-vengeance progressive pop tracks. Joining forces yet again with her musical buddy Jack Antonoff, plus Swedish pop machines Max Martin, Shellback, Oscar Görrer, Oscar Holter and Ilya, Taylor also collaborated with Ed Sheeran and Future for the track 'End Game'. Not only this, she sought the help of Richard and Fred Fairbrass and Rob Manzoli, otherwise known as the English pop band Right Said Fred, to sprinkle their musical insight onto 'Look What You Made Me Do' – the previously mentioned revenge single that would also go on to be the most popular song on *reputation*.

If you're looking through Taylor's award archives, it was obvious that *reputation* was bound to make some noise. In fact, history repeated itself yet again and it ended up making quite a racket. From its Best Pop Vocal Album Grammy nomination to Best International Artist nomination at the ARIA Music Awards, *reputation* took home a *Billboard* Music Award for Top Selling Album, an American Music Award for Favourite Pop/Rock Album, a Libera Award for Independent Impact Album and a Japan Gold Disc Award for Best 3 Albums.

reputation was also a staple on a heap of 'Best Albums of 2017' lists. As well as being ranked number five by *TIME*, seventh by *Rolling Stone* and nineteenth by the *Independent*, Taylor's newspaper-esque album cover ironically found its home among a slew of publications and outlets. As for the money, Taylor laughed all the way to the bank. The *Reputation Tour*, which ran from May to

November 2018, amassed $345 million. At the time, it became the highest-grossing US tour in history (which has now been surpassed by Taylor's own *Eras Tour*). Plus, due to *reputation* earning the title of the Bestselling Album of 2017, Taylor reportedly earned $1.9 million in the first month and a half of its release. Oh, and her record sales, streaming and publishing royalties go beyond $10 million.

What defines the era?

Head to Urban Dictionary and ask 'what does it mean to be in your "reputation" era?' In words I couldn't put better myself, the answer you'll get is: 'When someone says they are "entering their reputation era", it basically means that they are about to cause a ruckus to save their character.

'They will get revenge, and glow from the inside out.'

It essentially means you've shed your good-girl image and taken on your darker, more vengeful alter ego – but only because it was necessary and you needed to reclaim your truth and power.

reputation was the first time in Taylor's – at that point – 11-year career, where she went rogue and ditched the pure image she'd always worked so hard to preserve. It wasn't necessarily a choice, but more of a necessity. Had the hounding negative press and 'bad reputation' they cultivated not been part of Taylor's narrative at the time, chances are her darker, edgier self would never have been revealed.

Despite being birthed from such a dark period (which, of course, was sprinkled with light in Taylor's personal life), *reputation* is a perfect representation of how to overcome intense scrutiny without breaking your spirit. I think for anyone going through tough times it can be an album of real healing and empowerment. Although the album is fixated on enemies, reputations and ferociously standing up for yourself, in the background there's a sweet budding romance that is able to bloom in spite of the unrest.

As Taylor so eloquently put it:

'It's an album about finding love throughout all the noise, and how it makes you feel when people are saying things about you that you feel aren't true. If you can find something real in spite of a bad reputation, isn't that what matters most?'

reputation was – and is – about personal growth and resilience. When applying it to yourself, it acts as a reminder that everyone has the power to transform and rise above any challenge that may befall them. Taylor wanted us to know that our mistakes and flaws don't define us.

'I went through some times when I didn't know if I was going to get to do this anymore,' she said at the opening night of the *Reputation Tour* in Glendale, Arizona. 'I wanted to send a message to you guys that if someone uses name-calling to bully you on social media, and even if a lot of people jump on board with it, that doesn't have to beat you. It can strengthen you instead.'

reputation outfit inspiration

Okay, so you're in your *reputation* era? Whether your ex-boyfriend is leaving a trail of (untrue) bad press behind you following your break-up, you're ready to be a good girl gone bad (but only for the right reasons) as Rihanna would say, or you're ready to call out your demeaning boss, you need to be dressed for the part.

You'll already know that everything needs to be darker. That means ditching the Hollywood red lips for a darker shade of maroon, practising your best smokey eye, whacking on a choker and embracing your inner Nineties Winona Ryder.

Your *reputation* fit needs to be edgier and grungier than anything Taylor had worn before, which means the classy co-ords are out, leather and lace are in. On stage, she kept things moody with snake motifs, knee-high boots and black sequinned bodysuits. Even Goth Taylor wasn't about to ditch her beloved sparkles.

When feeling particularly *reputation*-like, Taylor even added a sequinned hood to said bodysuits to give off a darker energy. Coupled with smoke machines and moody lighting, the silhouette can easily double as a Taylor-inspired Halloween look. So, if you've got World Tour reputation on the brain, let's recap the most important essentials:

INTENSE SMOKEY EYE MAKE-UP

BURGUNDY LIPS

'I MEAN BUSINESS' BLACK NINETIES PLATFORM BOOTS

SNAKE ARM BRACELETS – or any other way you can incorporate a snake into your outfit. My fave? The one-legged pantless red-and-black snake bodysuit. It's simply iconic. Or, pick up a black bodysuit with sequinned snakes on it (super-easy to find online) and pair with a black leather skirt.

BLACK SEQUINNED BODYSUITS – not your vibe? Anything black and sequined will be equally striking.

Now, as we know, Taylor was seldom seen in public during her *reputation* era unless she was performing, which makes her casual street-style look harder to source. However, thanks to the birth of Grunge Taylor – and the fact that she didn't ditch her autumn girlie oversized sweaters – it's a very handy fashion era to channel. Mainly because it's so popular generally right now.

Some of my favourite everyday grunge pieces that will perfectly replicate the *reputation* era include:

THE TRUSTY BLACK MESH TOP – from plain, long-sleeve and fitted, embellished with tiny rhinestones or complete with intricate embroidered detail, have a surf of the Web (and visit some of the vintage shops) and you'll be sure to find a style for you.

CROPPED CROCHET BLACK SWEATER – the bigger the crochet loops, the better.

PLATFORM BOOTS, A CLASSIC STRETCHY CHOKER NECKLACE AND BLACK COMBAT TROUSERS

LEATHER SKIRTS – skater style or maxi, it's up to you.

A BLACK LACE TRANSPARENT BLOUSE WITH LONG STATEMENT SLEEVES – only do up one button of this as you'll either want to wear a sultry black or dark red slip dress underneath, or put on over the top of a crop top/bandeau and pair with combats.

Basically, so long as you're looking as grunge and vengeful as Taylor did back in 2017, you've cracked the *reputation* look.

This bright-red drink is a sure-fire way to protect your reputation at your next Swiftie event. Making a classic Taylor-themed, this drink is simple to make and always a guaranteed crowd favourite.

BAD BLOOD

INGREDIENTS

Ice cubes
250ml tomato juice
50ml lemon juice
A dash of Worcestershire sauce
1 teaspoon of celery salt
Fresh ground pepper
2 dashes of hot sauce –
Tabasco or Cholula (or to your spice taste)
1 celery stick, to garnish
1 pickle spear, to garnish

METHOD

- Fill a tall glass with ice cubes and pour in the tomato juice and lemon juice.

- Mix well.

- Add the Worcestershire sauce, celery salt, pepper and hot sauce to taste.

- Stir gently.

- Serve garnished with the celery stick and pickle spear.

7.

Lover
(2019)

Dripping in pastel colours and rainbows and oozing the dreamiest vibe, aesthetically, *Lover* is an era that makes you feel like you're living in the Care Bear land, Care-a-Lot.

Considering the edgy theatrics and grunge-filled *reputation* era, *Lover* was a huge shock to fans but in the best way possible. As quickly as she'd embraced her cloak-and-dagger demeanour, the singer discarded her matching maroon lipstick for the effervescent burst of colour and brightness that was Taylor Swift 2019.

It wasn't just a huge 180 visually, mind. With all of the quirk and candyfloss came Taylor's 'love letter to love', a bouncy synth-pop album brimming with upbeat riffs, atmospheric synthesisers and acoustic instruments. Despite being characterised and marketed as pop, *Lover* swam in a sea of eclectic styles, from bubblegum pop, funk and folk, and even gave a nod to Taylor's beloved country roots for the first time in two eras.

Lover was the first album that Taylor released with Republic Recordings and it was the first where she fully owned her master recordings. This was due to her signing with a new label following Ithaca Holdings and the music manager Scooter Braun purchasing Big Machine records – which, as we know, gave him ownership of her old masters. Taylor publicly called the situation her 'worst-case scenario', which is when she announced that she would be re-recording all her old albums. Since that point, the camaraderie has been unmatched, with fans worldwide rushing to purchase every single *Taylor's Version* released to date.

The *New York Times* labelled Taylor's strategy and the fallout as 'The Pop Music Civil War of 2019'. However, for Taylor, and the future of other artists, it was a major win because it addressed the long-accepted music ownership and distribution problem. Thanks to Taylor's fierce self-advocation during this time, the movement has been cemented as a formidable element of *Lover*. Which, as bubblegummy and starry-eyed as the era is packaged, is also filled with serious and culture-changing moments.

When looking at the lead single, 'ME!', which featured Panic! At The Disco's Brendon Urie, it's easy to get lost in the brightness and cheeriness of the track. The mid-tempo pop feel and catchy riffs are an instant smile facilitator, which is only heightened by the music video.

Because it was the lead single, Taylor was sure to include some sort of Easter egg or acknowledgement that she was through with her *reputation* era and ready to embrace love. She was, at this point, in one of the healthiest relationships of her adult life. Sure enough, the beginning of the video features a pink snake slithering on a multi-coloured brick road, hissing and harassing the camera – a clear reference to the snake-filled visuals of *reputation*. However, it suddenly implodes into a flurry of pastel butterflies, which fly off into the distance. Instantly, viewers are greeted with a visual representation of 'bye bye, Revenge Taylor' and 'hello, I'm in a Much Better Mood Taylor' – a direct quote from her 2019 appearance on *The Graham Norton Show* when she was asked to summarise her new bright pop aesthetic.

Such a palpable aesthetic change is noticed just as powerfully in the optimistic titular track 'Lover'. To Swifties everywhere, it signalled that perhaps the old Taylor wasn't dead, she was merely hibernating inside a snowglobe. Once again, Taylor declared that she would be 'overdramatic and true' to her lover, which welcomed back her self-deprecating but hedonistic character in true Swift style.

The lyrics in 'Daylight' could be the biggest giveaway as to how Taylor wanted her *Lover* era to pan out, though. She confessed that all she wanted in this life was to be defined by the things she loves and not by the things she hates, she's afraid of, or that haunt her. It seems her previous beliefs of love being 'burning red' weren't true – but they were, in fact, 'golden'. Again, fans were witnessing her rise from the *reputation* ashes, now experiencing the world through a colourful kaleidoscopic lens.

I will say one thing about Taylor: every album seems to house its own 'first'. With each era comes something Taylor smashes for the first time.

In *Lover*'s case, it was political activism. You couldn't miss Taylor when she entered 2019 – partly due to the spectrum of colours she exploded back onto the scene with – so it was no surprise that she made just as much of a spectacle when marching headfirst into her campaigning era. The most obvious example of her activism was with the anthemic 'You Need to Calm Down', a bright, summery, upbeat electropop song advocating for LGBTQ+ rights. It was the first time Taylor had released a track that resembled any kind of political statement and people were *listening*.

According to Taylor, the song is split into three sections, which she addressed during an interview with *Vogue*. She outlined that the 'first verse is about trolls and cancel culture', the second calls out 'homophobes and the people picketing outside our concerts' and the third references 'successful women being pitted against each other'.

Like any other Taylor song with a strong message, she dropped an equally compelling music video, which, of course, she co-directed. The video featured a huge number of celebrity cameos, both allies and members of the LGBTQ+ community. A slew of iconic drag queens and alumni of *RuPaul's Drag Race* were also invited to star during the third verse, where they impersonated female recording artists.

As such, the video was praised for its message while Taylor was commended for her activism, which led to many publications speaking out in support – from the *New York Times*, CNN and the *Irish Times* to the *Washington Post*, who noted that it was Taylor's most political move ever. The former's Jon Caramanica deemed her inclusion of the LGBTQ+ community 'a worthy celebration'.

But Taylor didn't just sing about these issues, she also used her platform – and her wealth – to action change. In April 2019, she donated $113,000 to the Tennessee Equality Project, which advocates for LGBTQ+ rights following the raft of anti-LGBTQ+ bills in Tennessee. Taylor took her actioning further, by creating her own petition in support of the Equality Act, which had been passed by the House of Representatives but was waiting to be brought for a vote in the Senate. She referenced the act in the 'You Need to Calm Down' video, which ended by asking her followers to sign the petition and support the legislation. Thanks to Taylor's world platform, it received over 800,000 signatures, surpassing her original goal of 300,000.

To this day, 'You Need to Calm Down' is regarded as a gay anthem and has achieved plenty of acclaim worldwide. It reached the Top Five in the UK, Australia, New Zealand, Canada, Ireland and Malaysia and landed the Number-Two spot in Scotland. The single also debuted at Number Two on the US *Billboard* Hot 100, which made it Taylor's second consecutive top-two single from *Lover*. This feat saw her knock Madonna off the top spot for the most Number-Two songs from a female artist in *Billboard*'s history.

Meanwhile, on Taylor's activism journey, 2019 was the year she dropped her Netflix documentary, *Miss Americana*, which took its name from the album's track 'Miss Americana & the Heartbreak Prince'. The streaming platform described the film as a 'raw and emotionally revealing look' at Taylor 'during a transformational period in her life as she learns to embrace her role not only as a songwriter and performer, but as a woman harnessing the full power of her voice'.

Too right – as well as documenting the creation of *Lover*, and reflecting on her songwriting process *and* rise to fame, the Netflix special marked Taylor's decision to go public with her political views.

While it may feel like Taylor was shunned by the Recording Academy during her *Lover* era (she was nominated for three Grammys but failed to scoop any of them), she did win big at the MTV Video Music Awards. There, she bagged three awards: Video of the Year and Video for Good with 'You Need to Calm Down' and Best Visual Effects for 'ME!' featuring Panic! At the Disco's Brandon Urie. *Lover* also won the favourite Pop/Rock album at the American Music Awards. Plus, it was the only album of 2019 that sold 1 million 'pure' copies, which means digital and physical sales. Then, as the American Music Awards crowned Taylor Artist of the Decade, *Billboard* took it up a notch and named her Woman of the Decade. Taylor's acceptance speech for the former was particularly poignant:

'This is an award that celebrates a decade of hard work and heart and fun and memories. All any of the artists or anyone in this room wants is to create something that will last, whatever it is in life. All that matters to me is the memories that I've had with you, the fans, over the years. Thank you for being the reason why I am on this stage. May it continue.'

However, the overarching cultural achievements of *Lover* are – and remain to this day – the biggest wins of all.

Talking of achievements, Taylor's *Lover* era marked a huge surge in popularity on social media. Loved-up Instagrammers everywhere would caption their romantic photo dumps with her famous 'three summers' lyric. From cutesy summer selfies to anniversary carousels, the lyric was a perfect, all-encompassing phrase that seemed like it was created for such an assignment.

While *Lover* acted as Gen Z's answer to Britney Spears's 'Born to Make You Happy' for millennials, Taylor's album track 'Cruel Summer' also had its own moment – albeit a few years after the album dropped. Fans had long said that the track, written alongside Jack Antonoff and Annie Clark (otherwise known as St Vincent), deserved to be a single but thanks to a ferociously viral TikTok trend that was launched off the back of the first leg of Taylor's *Eras Tour*, it ended up at the top of the *Billboard* Hot 100 in 2023.

When Taylor embarked on the tour in March 2023, fans were greeted with 'Cruel Summer' as the first song of the 44-track show. Away from the stadium, the Swiftie fandom created a dance that synced up to the song's bridge, which generated *thousands upon thousands* of original videos. Gigi Hadid even jumped on the trend – a major moment for Swifties considering their closeness during Taylor's *1989* era.

Following such a wild resurgence, *Rolling Stone* reported that just one month into touring, the track's average daily streams had skyrocketed by 120 per cent. And while at one of her June 2023 stops on the tour, Taylor gushed: 'The weirdest, most magical thing is happening,' as she announced 'Cruel Summer' as her next single.

During this era, Taylor was also scheduled to embark on her new creation: Lover Fest, a tour that would see her performing the album in a completely different format to her previous stadium world tours. Taylor's concept was to take *Lover* to four stadiums, plus pluck a hand-picked line-up of American artists to perform the European festival circuit in the summer of 2020.

Due to the pandemic, Taylor ended up having to pull the idea entirely, rather than reschedule. She shared her disappointment with her fans, noting that *Lover* really felt like her chance to do the things she 'hadn't done before, like Glastonbury'.

'I feel like I haven't done festivals, really, since early in my career – they're fun and bring people together in a really cool way,' she said upon news of the cancellation.

What defines the era?

Firstly, the *Lover* era was all about colour. After expressing her tumultuous press experience during *reputation* with an edgy, avenging vibe and darker pop elements like dubstep, *Lover* was the opposite. It felt like being inside a huge bubblegum bubble where everyone was celebrated no matter who they were or where they were from. And the electropop, sunshiney production made for an album that oozed hopefulness and positivity.

When someone says they are entering their *Lover* era, it means they're going through or have overcome the process of relearning what real, solid, good love should feel like. Your *Lover* era means you're in a happy state of self-growth and self-appreciation, and that you've finally found the courage to love yourself. And maybe that special someone as well.

In terms of what defines *Lover* for Taylor is her ceasing to rest, even though she was by now one of the biggest pop titans in the world. Rather than retreat into her love-filled bubble completely, she ended the decade more empowered and empowering than she had ever been. Using her industry experience to take back control of her music and career, while simultaneously leading the pack for artists present and future, Taylor fought for the rights she wished she'd had when she was coming up in the music world. Her relentlessness catapulted her to figurehead status, responsible for instigating change and being fearless enough to take on the challenge.

Lover was further defined by Taylor stepping into her activism shoes in her pastel-fuelled glory and using her voice to fight for minority communities. Her voice was loud, she was proud, and she was joined by a new squad who were all advocating for the same thing: equality.

'Rights are being stripped from basically everyone who isn't a straight white cisgender male,' Taylor said at the time. 'I didn't realise until recently that I could advocate for a community that I'm not a part of. It's hard to know how to do that without being so fearful of making a mistake that you just freeze. Because my mistakes are very loud. When I make a mistake, it echoes through the canyons of the world. It's clickbait, and it's a part of my life story, and it's a part of my career arc.'

At its core, *Lover* was all about spreading the love.

Lover outfit inspiration

With optimism, love spreading and being *in* love comes bright colours and a more playful wardrobe. If *reputation* was Taylor's Nineties grunge era, then *Lover* was most certainly her Seventies dreamscape era. Out went the black platform boots and in came the fringe, sparkles and pastel-coloured oversized suits. So, let's get right to it. If you're planning on bursting with love, pride and good vibes at the *Eras* concert (and all the time), you're definitely going to want to *Lover* it up.

Firstly, you simply cannot neglect the pastel colour palette. Especially not Taylor's trusty candyfloss pink. You're also going to want to reach for sky blue, lavender and light yellow to complete the set.

I'm going to start with make-up because, honestly, you can have so much fun with it during this era. Here's a list of essentials you'll need to stock up on and have in your cosmetics bag:

PASTEL-COLOURED EYESHADOWS

A SOFT PINK BLUSH

WHITE EYELINER

SMALL PINK STICK-ON LOVE HEARTS

For a super *Lovery* eyeshadow look, there are a few ways to go about it. To create a bold block-colour statement option, choose your favourite shade and swipe over your eyelid. You'll want to make sure that you keep the rest of your make-up minimal as the focus is on the eyes.

Alternatively, you could stick to the lavender and pink but create a smokey-eye pastel variation of purple. Start with the pink in the corners of the eye and then blend in the purple as you get to the middle and outer parts of the eyelid and below the brow bone. To make this look pop even more, add a subtle layer of the purple eyeshadow to the bottom lashes.

For the ultimate *Lover* unicorn-dream frosted eyeshadow, use a palette consisting of contrasting blue, green and purple shades. The blue belongs in the corner of the eye, while the middle of the lid is separated by the greeny-yellow hue. Use your purple eyeshadow to complete the rest of the lid, which should be smudged subtly again up to your brow bone. Finally, add some of the blue to your under-eye, as in the previous tutorial. Just a heads-up: you can also add a line of white eyeliner to your water line to make your eyes really stand out.

For extra head-turning points, add a subtle hint of pink blush to your cheeks and use the glitter hearts to create Taylor's iconic *Lover* heart eye. With the white eyeliner, draw a heart around whichever eye you prefer – preferably the same size as Taylor's. This will act as your stencil as you pop the stickers in place around it.

Now, let's move on to hair. For any *Lover* fanatic, you'll know that Taylor didn't just introduce the pastels to her cosmetics bags and wardrobe. She also, quite literally, dipped her locks into the theme. From pink and blue ombré tips to a brighter and sunnier blonde, everything about Taylor's *Lover* hair screamed festival vibes.

One thing I will say: if you're going to DIY but you're not one for switching your hair up massively, you may want to put the permanent dye down and pick up a semi-permanent one. Or, if even that's too much for you, I have two more options: grab a bottle of blue or pink shampoo and wash your hair with it to give the desired look without having to commit full-time. Or, order some temporary hair colour sprays online and just spray the tips of your hair. For full effect, and to avoid a harsh block of two separate colours, hold the can the furthest away that you can, and at the highest point. As you get to the middle and ends of the hair, gradually move the can and spray closer so you get a more gradual, gradient result.

Okay, lovers, now we've sorted your make-up and hair, let's decide what you're gonna wear. If you fancy the oversized pastel suit, get yourself back to the charity shops.

Oversized suits not your thing? I'd also recommend a pastel tie-dye rainbow two-piece with tons of fringing. Or, how about a blue-and-gold rhinestone bodysuit with matching silver sparkly boots? Too exposed? You could opt for a silver sparkly blazer dress with a pair of glittery fishnets and the aforementioned boots to make you look and *feel* like the man.

Another top choice (that can easily be recycled for a night out) consists of a long-sleeved pink sequinned minidress with a matching rhinestone clutch. Extra points for pastel-pink dip-dyed hair and a pair of pink metallic platform ankle boots.

Lover is *such* a strong era aesthetically. Not only will heads turn *and* roll, but there's also no doubt that you'll bring (and trail behind you) all of the smiles and rainbow feels.

If *Lover* is your go-to era, the below drink will fully encapsulate the fun and bright colours and feelings behind the iconic album. Make sure to have your favourite songs from the album on full blast while sipping away.

AFTERGLOW

INGREDIENTS

Crushed ice
60ml blue curaçao syrup
25ml lemon juice
25ml orange juice
200ml lemon-lime seltzer
Lemon and orange slice, to garnish

METHOD

- Fill a tall glass two-thirds full with crushed ice.

- Drizzle blue curaçao syrup into the glass.

- Add the lemon and orange juice.

- Stir well.

- Top with the lemon-lime seltzer and stir well.

- Serve garnished with a lemon and orange slice.

8.

folklore
(2020)

We open this era with an Easter egg: in April 2020, Taylor casually took to Instagram to post a selfie alongside the caption, 'Not a lot going on at the moment.' All Swifties know that this is a phrase significant to Taylor: remember, during the music video for Red's '22' she wore a T-shirt with the exact same words on it? It was a stage outfit during her tour too.

Taylor dropped the selfie at the beginning of a global pandemic, so for many, it rang true. Perhaps Taylor Swift, one of the most famous women on the planet with one of the busiest calendars and schedules *ever*, didn't have a lot going on at that exact moment either, just like the rest of us. Her famous phrase just happened to reflect life everywhere at that time, so what better opportunity to dig it up from the archives?

While at first many did brush off the generic addition to her grid as a direct response to 2020, it wasn't long until we all learned that it was, in fact, code. Three months later, in July, Taylor began posting a jigsaw puzzle of black-and-white, grainy images, much to her fans' confusion and intrigue. When the last image dropped, which completed a film shot of Taylor standing in a forest and looking up at the sky, it was quite obvious that something *huge* was around the corner.

Within hours of the final piece finishing the puzzle, Taylor announced that she *did* have a lot going on at the moment. She'd been busy working away in isolation on her eighth studio album, *folklore*, and it was set to be released at midnight.

'Most of the things I had planned this summer didn't end up happening,' Taylor captioned the post, referencing the shelving of her Lover Fest tour. 'But there is something I hadn't planned on that DID happen. And that thing is my 8th studio album, *folklore*. Surprise.

'I'll be releasing my entire brand new album of songs I've poured all of my whims, dreams, fears and musings into. I wrote and recorded this music in isolation but got to collaborate with some musical heroes of mine.'

She was talking about Aaron Dessner, the founding member of the rock band The National, Jack Antonoff, who she described as 'basically musical family at this point', and alternative indie outfit Bon Iver, 'who co-wrote and was kind enough to sing on one with me'. Plus, a certain Mr William Bowery, who as we all now know was Joe Alwyn's (her partner at the time) alias.

Due to the COVID restrictions in place at that time, Taylor built a home studio at her LA pad with the help of her engineer, Laura Sisk. Aptly titled 'Kitty Committee', it was where Taylor operated solely from in 2020, while her collaborators were scattered all over the US.

The unbelievable announcement marked two more firsts for Taylor: it was her first ever secret album, which apparently her label – Republic Records – weren't even aware of until the announcement, and the start of the transition into her alternative pop-folk era.

Without even listening to the record, you can tell it's a major shift from *Lover*. The pastel colour scheme was swapped for a woodsy, cottage-core aesthetic, which could only mean one thing: indie-folk star Taylor had arrived and was about to take you on a new musical journey. Another tick on the multi-music genre-domination list for Taylor and a glimmering light of hope for Swifties gutted that the pandemic had interfered with her original plans – 2020 was gearing up to be quite special in some ways, after all.

Upon the release of *folklore*, it was clear that Taylor had just dropped an emotionally intense album that would take more than one listen to dig deep into its meaning. Woven around the classic folk-style storytelling, Taylor explained that she explored themes of romanticism, escapism, empathy and nostalgia, and drew on fictional narratives and story arcs, and based the majority of the songs on a set of characters rather than her traditional autobiographical nature. As Taylor wrote in an elegant primer to accompany the release:

'In isolation my imagination has run wild and this album is the result, a collection of songs and stories that flowed like a stream of consciousness. Picking up a pen was my way of escaping into fantasy, history, and memory. I've told these stories to the best of my ability with all the love, wonder and whimsy they deserve.'

The short essay also explained how the images in Taylor's head soon 'grew faces or names and became characters'. She found herself 'not only writing [her] own stories', but also 'writing about or from the perspective of people' she's never met, people she's known and even those she wishes she hadn't.

Taylor described an exiled man 'walking the bluffs of a land that isn't his own, wondering how it all went so terribly, terribly wrong'. She told the story of an 'embittered tormentor showing up at the funeral of his fallen object of obsession'. The album observed 'a seventeen-year-old standing on a porch, learning to apologise' and 'lovestruck kids wandering up and down the evergreen High Line' – a public park built on a freight rail line above the streets on Manhattan's West Side.

More wholesomely, Taylor detailed the past of her grandfather, Dean, who landed at Guadalcanal in 1942, while a 'misfit widow' sought 'gleeful revenge on the town that cast her out'.

Even though many of the characters were imaginary, Taylor

did continue the sweet tradition of incorporating her close friends Blake Lively and Ryan Reynolds's children into her songs. Let me take you back a few eras for a minute to explain: almost two years after Taylor and Blake became friends following their first meeting at the Warner Bros. Movie World theme park in Queensland, Australia, she featured the famous couple's eldest daughter, James, on her *reputation* track 'Gorgeous'. If you listen again, you'll hear the then-two-year-old say the word 'gorgeous' before Taylor breaks into song.

Which now leads us to *folklore*, when James, plus her younger sisters, Inez and Betty, were name-checked during the song 'betty'. Ryan Reynolds spoke openly about how flattered he and Blake were when Taylor decided to use all three of their daughters in the track while talking to Jess Cagle at a SiriusXM Town Hall event in 2021: 'The names are the names of our kids, but you know, we trust her implicitly and she's very sensitive to any of that stuff ... We thought it was pretty, pretty damn amazing. We still do,' he continued, before adding, 'You know, I still walk down the street and shake my head, thinking: "I can't believe that happened."'

Elsewhere, Taylor and Blake's friendship crossed over into professional territory when, following the release of *Red (Taylor's Version)*, it was revealed that the *Gossip Girl* star had entered her own directorial debut era. Taylor's vault track 'I Bet You Think About Me' was directed by Blake and ended up being nominated for Video of the Year at the 2022 Academy of Country Music Awards and Music Video of the Year at the Country Music Association Awards.

During a time that was so uncertain, and when stories and imagination were required for many to see them through, Taylor told her community that a 'tale that becomes folklore is one that is passed down and whispered around'. Sometimes sung about, she was inviting people into her new world, which blurred the 'lines between fantasy and reality' and the 'boundaries between truth and fiction', which can 'become almost indiscernible'.

'Speculation, over time, becomes fact. Myths, ghost stories and fables. Fairytales and parables. Gossip and legend. Someone's secrets written in the sky for all to behold,' she wrote.

Such eloquence is expected of Taylor, but it's the wisdom she shares through *folklore*, as if she has glided through past lives with a floral-scented notepad and documented the existence of every person she met, absorbing each story as if it was her own, that sets this album apart from her previous ones. It acts as proof that the power of storytelling is 100 times *more* powerful when a true storyteller is the narrator.

During the release of the music video for the first single 'cardigan', Taylor joined some of her fans on YouTube to chat about the track, answer some questions and unpack the new album. She had already revealed that three of the songs on it were linked through the same concept, which she coined as 'The Teenage Love Triangle'.

At one point in the interactive YouTube session, Taylor revealed that one thing she did 'purposely' was 'put the Easter eggs in the lyrics, more than just the videos': 'I created character arcs and recurring themes that map out who is singing about who.'

After analysing deeply, many fans were convinced that these three tracks were, of course, 'cardigan', plus 'betty', which was inspired compositionally by Bob Dylan's 1963 and 1967 albums, *The Freewheelin' Bob Dylan* and *John Wesley Harding*, and 'august'. Describing the teenage triangle, Taylor added: 'These three songs explore a love triangle from all three people's perspectives at different times in their lives.'

TIME Magazine picked up on these interweaving hidden surprises, too, noting, 'Every song has these kinds of lyrical winks, reinforcing the universe that Swift has crafted even as she expands it with her newfound layers of fantasy and character.'

When looking at 'the last great american dynasty', which depicted the aforementioned 'misfit' woman, professional Swiftie social media sleuths quickly realised that the song was about the American socialite and composer Rebekah Harkness, also the previous owner of Taylor's sprawling Rhode Island home, and their similarities. Rebekah was a St Louis heiress and divorcée who got hitched to William 'Bill' Hale Harkness, heir to the Standard Oil fortune. They purchased the Rhode Island home and, in the song, named it 'Holiday House'. However, Bill died of a heart attack in 1954, leaving his estate to Rebekah. According to the *New York Times*, Taylor's lyrics concerning Rebekah's life are historically accurate.

As the song depicts, in the years after her husband's death, Rebekah did in fact have a great time doing whatever she wanted. From filling the pool with champagne to dyeing the neighbour's dog 'key lime green'. Like Rebekah, Taylor throws lavish Fourth of July parties complete with VIP and celebrity guest lists that make major headlines. She also likened her own famous girl squad to Rebekah's friends from the city, who most notably included bohemian artists Salvador Dalí and Andy Warhol.

As well as producing such lyrical masterpieces crammed with comparisons to her own life, Taylor got deeply personal in 'my tears ricochet', which specifically details her stolen masters' heartache. Among the characters Taylor had created for *folklore*, there's also no doubt that tracks like 'peace' and 'invisible string' were all about her relationship at the time. The latter indulged her fear of never being able to give her partner peace because of her spotlighted life.

Such dedication, imagination and divisiveness in each story is one of Taylor's true gifts and it's a unique quality that she bestows. But without the inspiration from other indie folk artists like Sufjan Stevens, Phoebe Bridgers and Lana Del Rey, *folklore* wouldn't have been able to encapsulate the essence of the genre as well as it did.

These influences, coupled with the album's indie-head collaborations, were a nod to the other artists she'd set her sights on to work with in the future. They also helped Taylor achieve the deep-rooted melancholy and classic self-introspection of the genre musically, from its lo-fi production to its use of neoclassical instruments, ethereal strings, the Mellotron, throbbing percussion and pensive horns.

Due to the pandemic, the whole approach to *folklore* was completely different from any of Taylor's previous albums. Right from the start, Beth Garrabrant, the photographer responsible for the album's artwork, told *i-D* that Taylor had 'a clear idea of what she wanted for the album's visuals'. She recalled that 'Surrealist work' and 'imagery that toyed with human scale in nature' were initial concepts, as well as 'early autochromes, ambrotypes, and photo storybooks from the 1940s'. As such, Taylor and Beth worked exclusively to achieve the final vision, going at it from a DIY approach due to the pandemic restrictions. Everything from the packaging, album art and lyric videos was done back-to-basics, which marked a complete difference from the elaborate photo shoots of Taylor's past. Rather than having '100 people on set, commanding alongside other people in a very committee fashion', everything was left down to Taylor, from how she styled her hair to her make-up and wardrobe. According to Beth, all Taylor provided was a specific moodboard characterised by black, white and greyscale filters.

folklore took on a completely new trajectory to *Lover*, which made an activism statement, or *Red*, which spewed emotional intensity. Purely because it came at a time when Taylor had literally nothing to prove anymore as an artist. Her string of world records, overflowing awards shelves, millions of streams and a committed fan base meant that she had already cracked the industry.

The album exuded a quiet confidence, the kind you can only get from experience, and was overwhelmingly blasé in terms of needing to win anyone over. She even told Paul McCartney in her 2020 *Rolling Stone* interview that *folklore* allowed her to be completely free with her lyrics and use words that ordinarily wouldn't make the cut due to them not being radio-friendly. Describing them as 'bigger, flowerier' and 'prettier', Taylor sang words like divorcée, elegies and epiphany, simply because they 'sound beautiful'.

folklore became the first album of 2020 to sell 1 million copies. It also ended up outselling every other record released that year and gave Taylor her third Grammy Award for Album of the Year, which made her the first woman to score a hat-trick for the accolade. 'cardigan', 'the 1' and Bon Iver's 'exile' landed in the Top 10 on music charts in eight different countries, with the former becoming Taylor's sixth Number-One single on the US *Billboard* Hot 100. *folklore* was certified Platinum or higher in the UK, Australia, New Zealand, Denmark, Poland, Norway and the United States and also marked Taylor's seventh US *Billboard* 200 Number-One album.

Music critics were thoroughly on board with the new Taylor, too, with many welcoming her latest musical direction with open arms. The *Guardian*'s Laura Snapes described it as the 'most experimental yet cohesive' of all Taylor's works, while *Variety*'s

Chris Willman deemed it a 'first-rank album' and a 'serious act of sonic palette [sic] cleansing'. Meanwhile, Roisin O'Connor of the *Independent* praised Taylor's 'exquisite, piano-based poetry', as *Entertainment Weekly*'s Maura Johnston celebrated Taylor's 'bold move to challenge her audience'.

Surrounded by all of these accolades, Taylor still concentrated on her fans and found the perfect way to give them a piece of *folklore* virtually. On 25 November 2020, she dropped the documentary/musical *Folklore: The Long Pond Studio Sessions* on Disney+, where she performed tracks and discussed the making of the album.

folklore shows Taylor's love of music and proves how fascinated she is by all genres, paying homage to them in her own way through the creation of each album.

What defines the era?

Ultimately, *folklore* came at a time when everyone was in grave need of some sort of escapism. The album was cathartic, offering a fictional folklore-inspired world that listeners could dive into and explore. Taylor created such an array of characters that all had their own personalities, quirks and histories, for that very reason. They were complicated, beautiful and substantial enough to be believed in. Ultimately, these characters kept Taylor and her fans company during a time of such isolation.

folklore can also be defined by Taylor's sonic shift from the upbeat electro-pop flair of *Lover* to her more introspective, folky melancholia. Her unhurried folk pop saw Taylor embrace her alternative popstar and, for the first time, she was able to write an album solely for her, without thinking about the commercial repercussions.

As Taylor said to *Entertainment Weekly* in December 2020:

'Songwriting on this album is exactly the way that I would write if I considered nothing else other than, "What words do I want to write? What stories do I want to tell? What melodies do I want to sing? What production is essential to tell those stories?"'

In terms of Taylor's actions during her *folklore* era, she used her platform to support independent record stores during the pandemic. Following the release, she signed copies of the CD and gifted them to stores all over the US, including Nashville's Grimey's, where she had quietly covered the salaries and healthcare of their employees for three months. Another store, Reckless Records, told *Rolling Stone* that they sold the signed copies like normal CDs so they were able to make some money.

The Record Store Day partnership was essentially about giving struggling stores – which are so integral to a town's grassroots music scene – a boost during that time and was a way to drive traffic to help keep them afloat.

Maybe, as well as giving her a chance to explore her musical depths without any pressure, *folklore* was Taylor's way of offering solace to people through a difficult time. She tied her indie-folk masterpiece up with a ribbon and said: 'Here you are, I might not be able to change what's happening right now, but I thought I could help you through.'

folklore outfit inspiration

If cosy cardigans and plaid coats are your entire personality, there's nowhere else you should be looking than your *folklore* era.

Characterised as an understated, woodsy, prairie-esque masterpiece, Taylor's *folklore* vibe looks like it was lifted straight from a Vashti Bunyan album and plonked headfirst into the twenty-first century. For 2020 Taylor, it was all about the simplicity and subtlety.

To achieve such a low-key yet highly sought-after look, here are the essentials:

A PLAID COAT – make it oversized like Taylor's for extra points.

COSY CARDIGANS ARE CRUCIAL – you can't guarantee good weather all the time, but your *folklore* era does require a lot of frolicking in the woodlands. Sidenote: they don't need to be found under someone's bed.

A RUFFLED PRAIRIE DRESS – whites and creams are advised.

MARY JANE SHOES – the above colours work best.

GINGHAM DRESSES AND MIDISKIRTS – the more oversized the better. Movement is super important during the *folklore* era.

TAN SATCHEL BAG – this should house said floral-scented notepad for woodland inspiration.

CUTE SHORT-SLEEVED WHITE FRILLY BLOUSES

If you can't already tell, the colour scheme circa *folklore* is relatively earth-toned – think of it as an extension of the outdoors.

Probably the easiest thing about the *folklore* style is the hair and make-up because of the minimal effort they both require. The era saw Taylor go make-up-free most of the time, or opting for a dash of mascara and a peach-coloured lip balm. Of course, natural or not, she was always donning the fashionable rosy cheeks, thanks to spending copious amounts of time in Mother Nature.

I will say that it's totally okay if you don't feel comfortable going sans make-up so if you do want to do your own thing make-up-wise, don't let me stop you. Your *folklore* experience should be all about *your* story and creative expression.

To go with your minimal (or not) make-up look and whatever *folklore* piece you've chosen from the rack, it's time to get practising those messy milkmaid buns. Way easier than the classic milkmaid braids, all you need to do is section your hair into two and plait either side as normal. Then twist the plaits round in a circular motion with your fingers until they sort of resemble cinnamon buns and secure with some hair grips. Remember, neatness is not required here, so if you have some flyaway wispy bits, one side is slightly higher than the other, or you plaited more hair on one side than the other, it doesn't matter – it's going to be getting caught on branches and blown about in the wind, anyway.

9.

evermore
(2021)

On 10 December 2020, three days before Taylor's thirty-first birthday, she announced that she'd be releasing her ninth studio album and second surprise album, *evermore*. Throughout the day, Taylor posted nine photos to Instagram in the same way as she did with *folklore*, which, when viewed all together on her grid, made up the album cover. The image showed Taylor from behind, wearing a plaid Stella McCartney coat, her hair plaited in a loose braid and facing a forest.

To accompany the final image, Taylor wrote: 'I'm elated to tell you that my 9th studio album, and *folklore*'s sister record, will be out tonight at midnight eastern. It's called *evermore*.

'To put it plainly, we just couldn't stop writing songs. To try and put it more poetically, it feels like we were standing on the edge of the folklorian woods and had a choice: to turn and go back or to travel further into the forest of this music. We chose to wander deeper in,' she expanded.

When Taylor said 'we', she meant Aaron Dessner, her *folklore* collaborator and her now seemingly indie-folk soulmate.

'In the past I've always treated albums as one-off eras and moved onto planning the next one after an album was released,' Taylor continued. However, she said there was 'something different with *folklore*'. In making the album, she described the process to be more like she was 'returning' rather than 'departing', admitting that she adored the escapism she found in her 'imaginary/not imaginary tales'.

'I loved the ways you welcomed the dreamscapes and tragedies and epic tales of love lost and found into your lives so I just kept writing them,' she said.

Just hours later, Taylor dropped further *evermore* teasers to social media: this time, the album's back cover complete with the tracklist of 17 new songs. Alongside the image, which depicted

Taylor in the same outfit and wandering pensively through the woods, she gushed that ever since she was 13, she'd been excited to turn 31 because it's her lucky number backwards.

Directly addressing Swifties everywhere, Taylor revealed that the album was a surprise gift for her fans who have 'all been so caring, supportive and thoughtful' on her birthdays.

'This time I thought I would give you something,' she typed, adding: 'I also know this holiday season will be a lonely one for most of us and if there are any of you out there who turn to music to cope with missing loved ones the way I do, this is for you.'

evermore, the musical and visual extension of *folklore*, has since been dubbed its wintery twin. As Taylor explained, it was the first time she had doubled up on an era, which is *why* the two albums are often treated as one. Therefore, many parallels can be drawn. Taylor's description of *evermore* being the development of 'the folklorian woods' can be identified through the cottage-core, escapist world she created with *folklore*.

Meanwhile, *evermore* was Taylor's second opportunity, as she said, to give her folklorian fables more time and space to grow. She was able to lean in to her imagination once again without the fear of industry pressures and the result was just as ethereal, soft, slow and gentle as its counterpart.

Following on from their virtual lockdown sessions, Taylor and Aaron Dessner continued to work remotely. He would send over instrumental tracks and Taylor would reply with a full set of lyrics. It was almost as if the two had fashioned their own unique indie-folk conveyor belt where they could churn out hit after hit.

Elsewhere, Aaron labelled *evermore* as a 'weird avalanche' that snowballed from its predecessor. And with Taylor simultaneously acknowledging *folklore*'s success, it gave her the spark to explore her newfound alternative songwriting skills further, taking *evermore*'s journey on a more experimental musical path.

The whole album was again recorded in secrecy and was completed with a much smaller team compared to any of Taylor's previous records, bar *folklore*. Aaron either produced or co-produced all of the tracks except for 'gold rush', which was taken on by Taylor and Jack Antonoff.

Thematically, *evermore* has been stylised as an anthology of anecdotes about love, marriage, grief and infidelity, and exploring every human emotion. Taylor told Zane Lowe during an Apple Music interview that the album deals with 'endings of all sorts, sizes and shapes' and the invariable pain and phases of each narrative. But much like *folklore*, *evermore* wouldn't be the revered indie album it is today without the influence of not just Aaron Dessner, but other greats, including Haim, who featured on the track, 'no body, no crime'.

The rock band and sisters Este, Alana and Danielle have been monumental figures in Taylor's life since *1989* days, way back in 2014. Much like many friendships in the digital age, they got chatting over social media when both Taylor and Haim gushed over how much they loved each other's music. Fast forward a year and the siblings were part of Taylor's twenty-fifth birthday bash at the Jingle Ball, before they all headed to the 2015 Golden Globes together, rounded off with a luxe trip to Hawaii. Later that year, and after some well-deserved fun in the sun, the foursome got back to work as Haim provided the opening musical entertainment for Taylor's *1989 Tour*. More recently, the supergroup were reunited on-stage after Haim invited Taylor to perform at their London show in 2022. This was reciprocated once more as Haim headed back on tour with Taylor as one of her opening acts on the *Eras Tour*.

Another member of indie royalty who helped to complete *evermore* was Marcus Mumford. The lead singer of English folk-rock band Mumford & Sons provided backing vocals for the track 'cowboy like me'. And to complete the list of *evermore* contributors, how can we forget the genius of Bon Iver, who teamed up with Taylor for round two?

Speaking of Mr Justin Vernon, the musician played a much bigger part in the making of *evermore* and his musical prints are littered throughout the album. For example, he played the drums on 'closure' and 'cowboy like me', guitar and banjo on 'ivy' and offered his chilling falsetto on the title track, 'evermore', plus backing vocals on 'marjorie'. Interesting fact: this track was initially meant to be an instrumental precursor to 'peace'. However, after Aaron Dessner sent it to Taylor, she ended up scribbling down some lyrics about her maternal grandmother, Marjorie, who was a professional opera singer. Alongside the familial lyrics, Taylor also sent Aaron a folder of Marjorie's opera records, some of which found their way onto the song as samples. Other notable tracks include 'closure' and 'dorothea', because, legend has it, they weren't actually meant to be part of 'evermore'. Instead, Taylor had originally offered the songs to Big Red Machine, Aaron Dessner and Justin Vernon's group, before they were diverted back to Swift land. Taylor's self-created indie-folk era wouldn't be complete without a certain Mr William Bowery either, who returned to co-write three tracks: 'champagne problems', 'coney island' and 'evermore'.

Tracing back the origins of some of Taylor's songs is so interesting, and especially so with the story of 'willow', which is told so nonchalantly, purely because it amplifies Taylor's songwriting talent so brilliantly.

Aaron Dessner composed an instrumental track named 'westerly' as an ode to the location of Taylor's Rhode Island and 'the last great american dynasty' home. It was a casual piece of music that was sent to Taylor, just like any other song on the album, but was returned to him one hour later, fully formed as 'willow'. And the result of such broad, experimental and boundaryless collaborations? A blend of indie folk, alternative rock and chamber pop, characterised by a slew of different sonic styles. From lavish strings, fingerpicked guitars and sparse percussion reminiscent of such genres, 'evermore' cemented Taylor's reputation as a respected indie artist.

A respected indie artist who during her *evermore* era was recognised as one of the most exceptional artists of our time and of *all* time at the 2021 BRIT Awards, too. During the ceremony, Taylor was presented with the Global Icon Award, an accolade that is reserved for only the most prolific and extraordinary talents of each generation. Upon acceptance, she became the first female recipient, with previous winners including David Bowie, Elton John and Robbie Williams.

Taylor's acceptance speech was instant proof that she was worthy. While briefly taking time to express how making *folklore* and *evermore* was 'one of the most unique, cathartic, extraordinary experiences' of her life, she quickly turned to her fans to tell them how 'indebted to and grateful' she is to them. But the most poignant part was when she spoke directly to every budding artist who has 'goals and ambitions and dreams for themselves'.

Offering her wisdom and experience, while also giving her nod of approval that it's okay to be different and to strive for something great, Taylor said: 'I need you to hear me when I say there is no career path that comes free of negativity. If you're being met with resistance, that probably means that you're doing something new. If you're experiencing turbulence or pressure, that probably means you're rising.

'There might be times when you put your whole heart and soul into something and it is met with cynicism or scepticism,' she continued, urging everyone everywhere that you 'cannot let that crush you' and 'you have to let it fuel you' instead. Because, as Taylor said, we live in a world where 'anyone has the right to say anything that they want about you at any time', but 'you have the right to prove them wrong'.

It's clear that receiving this award was the highest career point during Taylor's *evermore* era, but it's also important to note the profound effect the album had on the music landscape. The album earned Taylor a second consecutive nomination for Album of the Year at the 65th Annual Grammy Awards and sold over a million copies in its first week.

evermore hit Number One in 10 countries: the UK, the US, Canada, Australia, New Zealand, Croatia, Argentina, Belgium, Portugal and Greece, and was Taylor's eighth consecutive *Billboard* 200 Number One. It also went on to become 2021's bestselling Americana and alternative music album in the UK and the US.

What defines the era?

At this point, her star seemed more like a galaxy of fluorescent lights amid a chain reaction, which showed no signs of stopping.

Taylor received an honorary Doctor of Fine Arts degree from New York University, where she was introduced by Jason King, the chair and associate professor of the Tisch School of the Arts. As well as 'bringing joy' to her 'hundreds of millions of fans around the world', he described Taylor as one of the 'bestselling artists in music history', who has 'crossed genres, demographics, age groups and borders of all kinds'.

Donning a traditional gown and cap, Taylor offered an enlightened and eloquent speech, in which she addressed the graduates as a 'patchwork quilt of those who have loved us, those who have believed in our futures, those who showed us empathy and kindness or told us the truth even when it wasn't easy to hear'. She also yet again defied her global mega-successful superstar status and insisted to everyone everywhere that she was just one of us: 'No matter how much you try to avoid being cringe, you will look back on your life and cringe retrospectively.'

Taylor's indie-girl era was also in full swing when she officially started to re-record and release her albums after she first made the announcement in 2019. She dropped *Fearless* and *Red (Taylor's Version)* in 2021, the latter seeing her direct and release the music video for 'All Too Well (10-Minute Version)' and subsequently winning the Best Music Video Grammy for *All Too Well: The Short Film*.

What stands out during the *evermore* era, is Taylor continuing her creative exploration and musical evolution. Reflecting her growth as an artist and a human being, she ran with the themes previously explored in *folklore* and expanded on them, while also broadening her pool of collaborators.

Finally, *evermore* was when the musical magic between Taylor and Aaron Dessner really came to light and marked a partnership that 10 years ago nobody would have expected to produce some of the most respected alternative music in modern history.

ALBUM STATS AND ACCOLADES

evermore

Release Date:
11 December 2020
Debut on *Billboard* 200:
Number One, four weeks
***Rolling Stone* Rating:** 4.5/5
Certified (RIAA):
One x Platinum

evermore outfit inspiration

If you're looking for a distinction between your *folklore* and *evermore* looks, remember that *evermore* is defined as the wintery twin. This means cosy turtlenecks, cable-knit sweaters and the addition of a burnt-orange baker-boy hat are essential. Even just for warmth.

evermore also saw Taylor channelling an Ivy League student from the Sixties so you'll need a couple of cardigan sets, pleated skirts, Capri pants and, of course, a trusty plaid coat.

You'll have noticed that the colour scheme was pretty similar, again leaning towards neutral, warm colours and earthy tones, so it's definitely possible to switch up items from the *folklore* era and turn them into an *evermore* style.

For long velvet hooded capes and a 'willow'-style uffled silk organza and lace maxidress, I will once again direct you to vintage stores. While not forgetting the wild and unruly braid, *evermore* can feel like a hug on a cold winter's day and simultaneously makes you feel as though you're in some kind of woodsy, folklorian parallel universe.

The below recipe is as tasty as it is gorgeous – featuring tonnes of warming flavours, it's the perfect winter drink. Add a touch of edible gold glitter to really make it shimmer.

GOLD DUST

INGREDIENTS

Crushed ice
50ml cranberry juice
50ml apple juice
25ml lemon juice
25ml maple syrup
50ml sparkling water
Cinnamon stick and edible gold glitter, to garnish

METHOD

- Fill a cocktail shaker two-thirds with crushed ice.

- Add the cranberry juice, apple juice, lemon juice and maple syrup to the shaker.

- Shake well.

- Strain into a tall glass two-thirds filled with ice.

- Top with sparkling water and mix.

- Add a cinnamon stick and sprinkle gold glitter on top to garnish.

10.

Midnights
(2022)

What do you do next when you're Taylor Swift, the pop-culture icon, whose last new music releases were two surprise albums in the space of one year? You drop another record two years later and announce it at the 2022 MTV Video Music Awards, of course.

Midnights was Taylor's tenth studio album and, so far, her final era. The collection of 13 songs is an ode to different aspects of her life and career, and incorporates elements of her past eras, all leading to this one. In this respect, *Midnights* can be looked at as another concept album and, to be honest, I can't think of a better way to celebrate record number 10 and a career spanning 15 years.

Instagram played a major part in the anticipatory launch of *Midnights* as Taylor took to the platform multiple times to tease and share information. On 29 August 2022, she dropped two photos: one of the album cover, showing a moody close-up image of her face, complete with midnight-blue eyeshadow and her classic red lip while holding up a lighter in front of her right cheek. The second depicted Taylor with her head down in a shadowy room, surrounded by Seventies furniture and props, which we now know set the scene for the heavily vintage-inspired aesthetic of the era. However, it was the accompanying words on the second snap that drew fans' attention, as they cryptically explained the ethos of the album: 'We lie awake in love and in fear, in turmoil and in tears. We stare at walls and drink until they speak back. We twist in our self-made cages and pray that we aren't – right this minute – about to make some fateful life-altering mistake'.

Taylor explained that *Midnights* is a musical collection that she penned in the middle of many different 'sleepless' nights and one that journeys through dreams, both sweet and terrifying: 'The floors we pace and the demons we face. For all of us who have tossed and turned and decided to keep the lanterns lit and go searching –

hoping that just maybe, when the clock strikes twelve ... we'll meet ourselves.'

To conclude, she left fans with a quote that, unbeknown to us at the time, would become significant within the era: 'Meet me at midnight ...'

Although Instagram played its part, Taylor took to TikTok to help launch each track on the album. She created a series entitled *Midnights Mayhem With Me*, which saw Taylor unveil each song one video at a time between September and October 2022. Using a bingo cage and numbered balls to call out each song title at random, she left the announcements 'to fate'. Whether staged or not, Taylor revealed that 'the first track' she was going to tell us about was number 13. 'Because of course,' she added, alluding to her lucky number.

The album explores the different aspects and reactions of a person's inner thoughts and feelings, from insecurity to anxiety, insomnia, self-confidence, self-deprecation, self-awareness and self-criticism. Taylor also set the record straight when she revealed that *Midnights* focuses on (and was inspired by) five major topics. She explained them as self-hatred, falling in love, falling apart, revenge fantasies and wondering what might have been.

To accompany these lyrical themes sonically, Taylor embarked on a major vibe shift from *folklore* and *evermore*, delving back into her pop roots. While *Midnights* is classed as a pop album, it's important to note it is very different to her previous pop offerings. By incorporating dream pop, bedroom pop, ambient pop, chilled-out pop, R&B and electronica, Taylor's blending of genres created an album that feels like an alternative approach to synth-pop.

Taylor continued to trickle surprises with the release of *Midnights*. One teaser included an Instagram video, labelled as the 'Midnights Manifest'. It was a calendar detailing events that were happening in relation to the record. However, if fans looked closely they were met with one 'special very chaotic surprise' that seemed to be more ambiguous than the rest. Set to take place on Friday, 21 October at 3 a.m. – three hours after the release of *Midnights* – Swifties soon deduced that there wouldn't be just 13 tracks. Rather, Taylor would be releasing seven more songs in the extended album version.

Sure enough, on that exact date and time, Taylor took to her grid once again to post another Seventies-esque shot of her wearing a plaid skirt while sitting on a wicker trunk and playing a vintage synth. Sharing that she, too, thinks of *Midnights* as a 'complete concept album, with those 13 songs forming a full picture of the intensities of that mystifying, mad hour', she also added that she had written other tracks on her 'journey to find that magic 13'.

Taylor referred to these songs as her '3am tracks' and added that she'd been 'loving the feeling' of sharing more of her and her collaborators' 'creative process', such as her 'From The Vault' offerings. These are previously unreleased songs written during the timeline of each album, but gifted to fans as a surprise later on during each 'Taylor's Version' drop. What's more, on the day the album came out – and prior to the announcement of the additional tracks – Taylor posted a carousel of photos of the making of the album. In the caption, she described *Midnights* as a 'wild ride' and said how she 'couldn't be happier that [her] co-pilot on this adventure' was Jack Antonoff.

'He's my friend for life and we've been making music together for nearly a decade HOWEVER ... this is our first album we've done with just the two of us as main collaborators,' she revealed.

Taylor delved into their experience of the album and shared that it 'coalesced and flowed' out of them. She recalled that they found themselves back in New York, where they would stay up late and record every night, while 'exploring old memories and midnights past'.

'*Midnights* is a collage of intensity, highs and lows and ebbs and flows. Life can be dark, starry, cloudy, terrifying, electrifying, hot, cold, romantic or lonely.'

After such an exciting musical moment for Taylor and her fans, she also had another little surprise waiting around the corner. Taylor wasn't dropping just one album cover for the vinyl version of the album, she was offering four. As an added layer for her fans, she later revealed that, when put together, the four different cover artworks made a clock to tie in with the theme of time.

With the help of Mr Antonoff, and Taylor's self-described 'brilliant collaborators', she made history after the album took all of the Top-10 spots on the *Billboard* Hot 100 song list. *Midnights* also made Taylor the first ever artist to achieve such a thing. Not only this, the album nabbed another Spotify record after it accomplished the most single-day streams of an album, while simultaneously topping the charts in 28 countries. And when talking about vinyl, *Midnights* sold the largest amount in one week in the US in the whole of the twenty-first century. It was also the bestselling album of 2022 in the United States.

During the making of the album, Taylor and Jack Antonoff were joined by a slew of other music industry heads. From Sam Dew, who has written for Rihanna, Kendrick Lamar and Mary J. Blige, to Mark Spears aka Sounwave, known for his work with

Chloe x Halle, Mac Miller and Bleachers, the duo also teamed up with Jahaan Sweet, who has produced for major names like Kehlani, Drake and Eminem. Elsewhere on the list of collaborators, and whom Taylor openly thanked, were producer Keanu Beats, her long-time engineer Laura Sisk, Zoë Kravitz and Lana Del Rey. And who can forget Aaron Dessner, who joined Taylor two years later to co-produce and co-write some of her bonus tracks?

As Taylor explained in an August 2022 Instagram post, *Midnights* is 'the stories of 13 sleepless nights scattered throughout my life', whether due to anxiety or adventure. When we look at the tracks from the album and dissect them further, it makes sense to start with the lead single, 'Anti-Hero'. Thanks to Taylor being so vocal about the track, we know that it's an overwhelming piece of music about one's insecurities and anxieties. Through such honest lyricism, we can hear her deal with her fears, doubting those she trusts and experiencing concern about pretty much everything. Contrastingly, she has described it as her favourite track on the album and one of her favourite songs she's ever written.

However, she explained her reasons on Instagram again. 'I struggle a lot with the idea that my life has become unmanageably sized, and not to sound too dark, but I struggle with the idea of not feeling like a person,' she added.

In fairness, whether you're a Swiftie or not, it is hard to imagine what life as Taylor Swift must be like. Many see her as a cultural figure, placed on this earth to entertain and serve, and so the lines can often be blurred between her own humanity and her extraordinary celebrity.

Taylor likened 'Anti-Hero' to a 'guided tour' through all of the things she, and we, dislike about ourselves. But things that we

'have to come to terms with' if we're ultimately going to be happy in the long run.

Another night of insomnia gave us the track 'Bejeweled', which details a person being frustrated with their lover because they're not valuing them as they should. To retaliate, the narrator declares that she's going on a night out and knows that she'll generate plenty of interest and sparkle in any room she steps into.

Alongside 'Anti-Hero', 'Bejeweled' is one of the standout tracks of *Midnights*, both in terms of the song and the music video. The latter is thanks to the Haim sisters appearing in the *Cinderella*-style video as Taylor's wicked step-sisters.

What was also really cool *and* completely Taylor Swift were the Easter eggs that were packed into the video. Most notably, the orchestral versions of the *Speak Now* tracks 'Enchanted' and 'Long Live' featured at the beginning and end, which alerted fans to the next re-release.

Next stop, 'Lavender Haze', as we can't *not* dig deep into the single that features backing vocals from Zoë Kravitz. The track and its equally romantic music video, written and directed by Taylor, reflects the lengths someone in love will go to in order to protect their privacy and relationship.

Apparently, Taylor stumbled across the Fifties' phrase 'lavender haze' while watching the TV drama *Mad Men*, and explained during her *Midnights Mayhem With Me* video series that she thought it was 'very beautiful'. Describing it as an 'all-encompassing love glow', to be in a 'lavender haze' means you're deeply in love with someone, or experiencing the whirlwind honeymoon stage.

'I guess, theoretically when you're in the lavender haze, you'll do anything to stay there and not let people bring you down off of that cloud,' she added during her explanation of the track.

Furthermore, in true Taylor fashion, the video was similarly littered with Easter eggs – hinting yet again at the release of *Speak Now (Taylor's Version)*. Remember the koi fish and purple theme of the third era? But it was also the first video Taylor wrote out of the first three she released and the one that helped her 'conceptualise the world and mood of *Midnights* like a sultry sleepless 70s fever dream'.

As for 'Snow on the Beach', it's all about 'falling in love with someone at the same time as they're falling in love with you in this sort of cataclysmic, fated moment where you realise someone feels exactly the same way that you feel' and was co-written with Lana Del Rey. This collaboration was one that fans couldn't get over, especially as Taylor has been so vocal about her love of Del Rey's music over the years. *Midnights* seems to be the perfect album for this partnership, too, thanks to the cinematic and retro atmosphere that is synonymous with Lana Del Rey. It was also a full-circle moment for both stars, as each has worked closely with Taylor's long-time musical partner, Jack Antonoff.

'I thought it was nice to be able to bridge that world,' the 'Born to Die' singer shared in a *Billboard* interview.

The *Guardian* described *Midnights* as 'a moody, sophisticated filter on the pop that made [Taylor's] name', while *Consequence* labelled it as a fusion of '*reputation*'s attitude, *1989*'s unimpeachable hooks, and *Lover*'s heart-on-its-sleeve vulnerability'.

What defines the album?

At first glance, it's easy to view *Midnights* as a return to Taylor's poppier discography after her grainy filtered, cabin-core eras of *folklore* and *evermore*. However, due to its embrace of different versions of pop and experimentation with new sounds – alongside the Seventies aesthetic – the album has landed itself in a league of its own entirely.

It's also hard not to view *Midnights* as Taylor's entry into an elite club of icons. In a 2023 poll undertaken by YouGov, Taylor Swift was the number-one most famous pop artist alive. She is only number two to Michael Jackson overall, but reigns supreme over iconic acts dead and alive, including Queen B herself, Prince, Lady Gaga, Elton John, Whitney Houston and Britney Spears.

This feat has undoubtedly been helped by her *Eras Tour*, which is Taylor's most expansive outing yet – and one that will surely be hard to beat. Setting off in March 2023, just five months after the release of *Midnights*, the tour has already made a momentous impact culturally, economically and politically, all of which have been demonstrated by the exceptional demand in ticket sales and records in venue attendance. Plus, the breaking of Ticketmaster and the boosting of business, tourism and economy in each of the cities in which Taylor performs. As of October 2023, the scale of its success pushed her net worth over the $1 billion mark, which made her the first-ever artist to accumulate such wealth with music as the main income source.

The *Eras Tour* far surpassed any other level of Taylor's previous tours and instantly became a cultural phenomenon, both in the physical world and on-screen. In fact, the demand became so huge and tickets became so hard to come by that Taylor had to make it exist in the virtual world, too. And no, these experiences weren't just through discovery pages on Instagram and TikTok, which featured livestreams, reactions and dissections of the show, but also the rollout of *Taylor Swift: The Eras Tour* concert film. This gave fans who weren't able to secure tickets the opportunity to witness the spectacle at the cinema. The fact that Taylor wasn't even halfway through the tour when the film was made is an anomaly in itself. Honestly, the scale of the demand is hard to comprehend.

Meanwhile, in the *Eras Tour* world, Taylor was not only being adored by her fans, but also being honoured by a multitude of cities around the US. It all started in Glendale, Arizona, when the city officially changed its name temporarily to 'Swift City' ahead of Taylor's arrival. Other parts of the US soon followed suit, with Arlington in Texas debuting a street called Taylor Swift Way and giving her a key to the city. Las Vegas illuminated its Archway Gates with images of all the eras, while in Tampa, Florida's mayor, Jane Castor, invited Taylor to be the city's honorary mayor for a day. Most wholesomely, though, Nashville renamed the Nissan Stadium *Eras Tour* as the Taylor Swift Homecoming Weekend. After all, the city was where it really all started for Taylor, so it was no surprise when Mayor John Cooper issued a statement welcoming her back.

Referencing her songs, he said: 'Long story short, Taylor Swift is a legendary musician, producer and director,' and, 'Karma is Taylor Swift coming straight home to Nashville to play three sold-out tour performances at Nissan stadium.'

As of August 2023, the *Eras Tour* was the highest-grossing tour ever by a female artist. When it ends, it's expected to be the highest-grossing concert tour of all time. This achievement is only heightened when you look at some of the figures from other incredibly successful female artists, whose concert tours – which once held the top spot – have now been surpassed by Taylor – the worldwide *Eras Tour* is estimated to make around £840,000,000. From Beyoncé's recent *Renaissance Tour*, which grossed $579,800,000, to Madonna's 2008–09 *Sticky and Sweet Tour*, which brought in $560,622,615, the number gap between theirs and Taylor's is quite staggering. Especially when you think that in November 2023, she was 60 shows down, but there'll be 151 performances in the bag when the *Eras Tour* wraps up in December 2024.

Midnights was also when Taylor's fully established social media ecosystem was at its most prosperous. Thanks to her TikTok series *Midnights Mayhem With Me*, and the multi-platform release schedule of the album, the *Atlantic* equated Taylor's social media hold to a 'true metaverse'. Dominating an immense social media community across a string of platforms, all of whom live in a Taylor Swift universe, the star is classed as an example of someone who has mastered all areas of fandom.

Because *Midnights* touches on each of Taylor's eras, spanning over 15 years, the album can be defined by her ability to hold attention. All despite her deep insecurities, presented in songs like 'Anti-Hero', as well as similar sentiments from her previous eras of feeling like she had to prove herself after the age of 22.

Taylor spoke to Jimmy Fallon of *The Tonight Show* during the week of *Midnights'* release about this exact issue, where she opened up about her conflicting feelings about being successful yet insecure: 'I'm feeling very overwhelmed by the fans' love for the record. I'm also feeling very soft and fragile. The two can exist at once,' she said at the time.

'But the fact that the fans have done this, like the breaking of the records and the going out to the stores and getting it ... I'm 32, so we're considered geriatric pop stars. They start to put us out to pasture at age 25. I'm just happy to be here.'

Whether Taylor's commitment to building her name in the film industry was part of her plan to stay relevant or reinvent herself is debatable, but it's definitely a big part of her *Midnights* era. In December 2022, she announced her feature directorial debut with the Academy Award and Golden Globe-winning Searchlight Pictures, alongside the news that she'd written an original script. Despite further news of her new career venture being kept hush-hush right now, Searchlight presidents David Greenbaum and Matthew Greenfield did express in a statement their elation at being able to work with 'a once-in-a-generation artist and storyteller'.

'It is a genuine joy and privilege to collaborate with her as she embarks on this exciting and new creative journey,' they added.

Of course, Taylor is no stranger to directing, having completed a string of her own music videos in *Midnights* and previous albums. A major moment that happened for the star during this era directorial-wise was the screening of her 14-minute production *All Too Well: The Short Film* at the 2022 Tribeca Film Festival and Toronto International Film Festival.

I simply can't close this final eras chapter without one of the most defining fan moments of *Midnights*. For the majority of us, the last time we got crafty with beads was way back in our childhoods, but upon the release of *Midnights*, and especially as the *Eras Tour* kicked off, Swifties brought back the beautiful trend of making friendship bracelets. Taking inspiration from the lyrics of 'You're On Your Own, Kid', fans began trading their colourful beaded creations as a staple activity ahead of the show. Of course, these bracelets – referencing anything from a Taylor song, to an era and even fan theories – soon found their way to social media and exploded in popularity in Taylor's 'virtual world'. So popular were they that celebs from Gigi Hadid, to Jennifer Lawrence and even Aaron Dessner were photographed swapping and accepting their own friendship bracelets. Naturally, it was no surprise when Taylor hopped on her own trend and took home bracelets made by her fans, too. This global movement was a visual representation of the positive universe Taylor has worked so hard to create, and at its core was friendship – *Midnights* just took it to the next level ...

MAKING FRIENDSHIP BRACELETS

You simply cannot rock up to any Taylor Swift-related outing, a themed party, the *Eras* concert movie or the *Eras Tour* itself without a friendship bracelet. At this point, it's classed as sacrilege. Besides, when I – or anyone else who doesn't live under a pop-culture rock – hears the words 'friendship bracelets', the first thing that springs to mind is no longer primary school or summer camp hobbies, it's Taylor Swift! So, what better T. Swift activity to pass the time than hosting your own friendship-bracelet-making session for your fellow Swifties?

This is an easy, low-cost crafting activity, so here's your ultimate guide on how to make the cutest friendship bracelets that will last a lifetime.

Things you'll need

- ♥ A pair of scissors

- ♥ Elastic cord string, typically 1mm thick

- ♥ Colourful large beads ranging in shape from stars and hearts to the classic round ones

- ♥ Lettered alphabet beads

How to make them

♥ Use the scissors to cut enough elastic to go around your wrist (wrap it round as a check) and so that you've got scope to be able to knot it a few times.

♥ Tie a knot at one end of your elastic – this is where your bracelet starts. Make sure the knot is big enough, tight enough and secure enough – you don't want the beads slipping off mid-thread.

♥ Depending on your design, get your beads ready in the order that you'll be threading them by laying them out on a table. Whether it's a song title, a song lyric or the name of your bestie, it's a good idea to do this first so you can see how it looks. Decorative beads either side of the lettered ones look great and they'll help to fill up the elastic if your phrase or word is too short.

♥ Thread the beads you have arranged in order onto the elastic and tie a knot at each end so they stay in place.

♥ Now, knot the two ends together to finish.

♥ Last, but not least, either try your friendship bracelet on and keep it, or swap it with your best pal.

For the ultimate Swiftie friendship-bracelet-making session, just make sure you're blasting out Taylor's entire discography at full volume while you work!

Midnights outfit inspiration

Taylor's *Midnights'* fashion epoch is riddled with Seventies nostalgia. Take a look at some of the earliest examples of her social media content promoting the album and you'll be greeted with velvet furniture, colour-blocked wallpaper and vertical wooden panelling, all of which are reminiscent of the era.

Vogue swiftly picked up on the Seventies feel of Taylor's fashion during this era, noting that it marked a turning point from her prairie-style *folklore* and *evermore* attire. Meanwhile, fashion critic Jess Cartner-Morley found similarities in Taylor's vision to English art-rock band Roxy Music's 1974 album, *Country Life*.

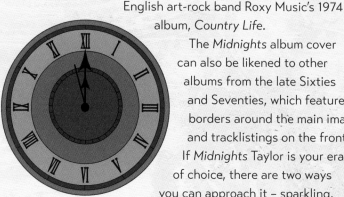

The *Midnights* album cover can also be likened to other albums from the late Sixties and Seventies, which featured borders around the main image and tracklistings on the front. If *Midnights* Taylor is your era of choice, there are two ways you can approach it – sparkling, bejewelled Taylor, or intimate, low-maintenance Taylor. Let's unpack them both.

Is the celestial-themed, midnight-blue satin one-piece she wore to the 2022 VMAs more your vibe? You're going to want to steer in this direction ...

SILVER SPARKLY
DRESSES, BODYSUITS
OR FLARED
TROUSERS – basically
anything that screams
disco-ball Seventies
fashion.

AN OVERSIZED
WHITE FAUX-FUR
SHAWL

OVERSIZED BLUE OR PURPLE FEATHER OR FAUX-FUR COATS – think of the 'Lavender Haze' music video and you've nailed it.

LOTS. OF. SILVER. BLING. When I say the blingier the better, I really mean it.

A NAVY VELVET MOON-PATTERNED, BELL-SLEEVED ROMPER DRESS

CHUNKY OPEN-TOE PLATFORM HEELS

A NAVY-BLUE TWO-PIECE – ideally a maxiskirt coupled with a matching roll-neck, long-sleeved top and littered with sparkles.

A MIDNIGHT-BLUE BODYSUIT *DRIPPING* IN SEQUINS

EXCESSIVE AMOUNTS OF BLUE, GLITTERY EYESHADOW – just look at the 'Bejeweled' video for inspiration *and* as a handy reference.

DON'T FORGET THE RED LIP

If you haven't caught on already, stage and awards *Midnights* Taylor prefers silvers, celestial colours and palettes that scream, 'I'm going out tonight.' Meanwhile, sipping coffee in the studio, day-to-day Taylor is a lot more subdued and in keeping with the album art. Here are the must-have items to achieve the look:

COSY, AUTUMNAL SHADES ARE EMBRACED YET AGAIN – think burnt orange, beige, deep greens, mustard and baby blue.

SEVENTIES PATTERNS LIKE STRIPES, LARGE FLOWERS, DOGTOOTH OR CHECKS

SHRUNKEN POLOS – any of the above colours are perfect.

WARM, RIBBED KNITS

ANYTHING CORDUROY

HIGH-WAISTED FLARED TROUSERS – great for creating a Seventies silhouette.

COLLARS ARE IN – Taylor's horizontal stripy sweater vest or her patchwork collared polo T-shirt in the 'Anti-Hero' music video are your reference points.

A PAIR OF CHUNKY LOAFERS

One final note before you either bejewel yourself into next year or cosy up in your orange ribbed jumper ... Both versions require a friendship bracelet, ideally one that you've made yourself and then swapped with your mates.

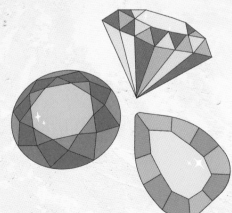

Are you prepping a *Midnights*-themed drink for your Taylor Swift party? This lavender-based cocktail is the perfect choice for you and your mates! If you'd really like it to ooze lavender, add a drop of purple food dye into your drink so it really looks the part.

LAVENDER HAZE

INGREDIENTS

Crushed ice
100ml fresh grapefruit juice
75ml lavender syrup
25ml grenadine
50ml soda water
1 fresh basil sprig, to garnish
1 fresh lavender sprig, to garnish

METHOD

• Fill a cocktail shaker two-thirds with ice, then add the grapefruit juice, lavender syrup and grenadine.

• Shake well.

• Strain into a tall glass two-thirds filled with crushed ice.

• Stir in the soda water.

• Serve garnished with the basil and lavender sprigs.

WHAT'S YOUR ERA?

One last round before we all apply for quiz shows with Taylor Swift as our expert subject. And to be honest, how could I not include a bunch of questions that celebrate why we're all here in the first place? That is, each of Taylor's magical, life-changing and defining eras, of course. So, with that, let's answer the burning question: *what's your era?*

How would you rather spend the summer?
A.   In New York
B.   A cabin in the woods somewhere
C.   In Nashville
D.   Chilling in your own home away from the cameras
E.   Campaigning for equality
F.   Writing songs with Ed Sheeran
G.   Why does it never snow on the beach?

How do you deal with a hard break-up?
A.   Hang out with your friends
B.   Write about a teenage love triangle to take your mind off things
C.   Write fairy-tale love stories to make yourself feel better
D.   Your alter ego takes their revenge
E.   Think of the positives and move on
F.   Never, ever get back together
G.   Dress up in your best bejewelled glam and go on a night out

What shoes do you feel the most comfortable in?

A.   A pair of strappy heels

B.   Some tan brogues

C.   A pair of cowboy boots

D.   Black Nineties platform boots

E.   Pink metallic ankle platform boots

F.   A pair of casual red pumps

G.   Chunky burgundy Seventies loafers

What colour palette do you vibe with the most?

A.   Blue and white

B.   Forest green and navy

C.   Purple

D.   Black and grey

E.   Pastel pinks and blues

F.   Just red

G.   Red, burgundy and burnt orange

What's the best song to shout the lyrics to?

A.   'Welcome to New York'

B.   'the last great american dynasty'

C.   'Better than Revenge'

D.   'This Is Why We Can't Have Nice Things'

E.   'You Need to Calm Down'

F.   'I Knew You Were Trouble'

G.   'Bejeweled'

What's your go-to hairstyle?

A. A straight bob

B. A wild, unruly braid

C. Big, bouncy curls

D. Slicked-back hair

E. Pastel-dipped dyed ends

F. Straight

G. Long, down and natural with a fringe

Which Track Five is your favourite out of the ones below?

A. 'All You Had to Do Was Stay'

B. 'my tears ricochet'

C. 'Dear John'

D. 'Delicate'

E. 'The Archer'

F. 'All Too Well'

G. 'You're On Your Own, Kid'

Which of these items is most likely to be found in your bedroom?

A. A Polaroid

B. A vintage tee and a brand-new phone

C. A purple guitar

D. Snake arm bracelets

E. A snow globe

F. A bowler hat

G. A Seventies synth

Out of these stories, which is your favourite?

A.   *Alice's Adventures in Wonderland*
B.   *The Great Gatsby*
C.   *Romeo and Juliet*
D.   *A Tale of Two Cities*
E.   *To All the Boys I've Loved Before*
F.   *The Hunger Games*
G.   *Jane Eyre*

How do you edit your Instagram photos?

A.   With a Polaroid filter
B.   A greyscale filter
C.   Sepia tones
D.   Black and white
E.   Pastel filter – lover
F.   Lots of saturation – the red needs to pop
G.   A grainy, Seventies retro

How would you describe love?

A.   Delicate
B.   Folklorian
C.   New
D.   Noisy
E.   Sweet
F.   Burning red
G.   Nostalgic

What's your idea of relaxing?

A. Hanging out with your girl squad

B. Reading a book by the fire

C. Writing your own fairy tale

D. Staying at home, away from the spotlight

E. Hanging out with your cats

F. Learning how to play the Appalachian dulcimer

G. Writing songs at midnight

Mostly As – *1989*

Your friends are your life and you're definitely the most empathetic and reliable of the group. You're also the person most likely to be clutching a Polaroid at all times during a social event because it's important for you to immortalise your memories with those closest to you.

Mostly Bs – *folklore/evermore*

While reading this, chances are you're pulling your chunkiest cardigan out from under the bed and planning on going for a walk in the woods to clear your head. You love getting lost in your own folklorian thoughts as it's your way of coping with things when life gets a little tough, but your real-life experiences have made you a stronger person and you're better for them. And breathe …

Mostly Cs – *Taylor Swift/Fearless/Speak Now*

Youthful optimism and a sprinkling of fairy-tale romance dominate your every waking moment and you just can't wait to meet 'The One'. Your journals are filled with thoughts about first kisses, first dates and happy endings, while your wardrobe is brimming with whimsical outfits that depict your very own love story.

Mostly Ds – *reputation*

Basically, no one messes with you, and second chances really aren't your thing. Only if someone has really hurt you, that is. Whatever rocks are thrown at you, you make a masterpiece out of them and come out the other side stronger and wiser than you were before.

Mostly Es – *Lover*

Right now, your life is filled with sunshine, rainbows and unicorns. You see the positives in everyone and everything, and you'll stop at nothing until equality and inclusivity are achieved for all. You know that you're the only one of you and you want to make your time in this world count.

Mostly Fs – *Red*

You're in your *Red* era and you're absolutely loving it. You're all about girls' trips and weekends away, and you're not gonna let a break-up get in the way of you having fun. In a nutshell, no one's going to push you around and they're certainly not going to kill your single vibe.

Mostly Gs – *Midnights*

Are you feeling pretty retrospective about your life right now? If so, you're definitely in your *Midnights* era. You're looking back at your memories through a retro Seventies lens, but rather than think about what you might have done differently, you're comfortable in your triumphs and your mistakes. You've come full circle and you're able to fully appreciate yourself for who you are. Love that for you!

Dear reader,
so, what is your era?

I hope you've enjoyed rediscovering each era as much as I have, from rummaging through the vaults of Taylor's early Nashville days to her country-pop crossover break-through, followed by the journey through an indie forest landscape and back out again.

Reading this back, it sounds as if Taylor should be in the same age bracket as veteran musical icons, from Cher to Diana Ross to The Beatles. Crossing and blurring so many genres and producing 10 albums to date (not to mention her re-recordings) – all of which have won accolades or broken some kind of world record – seem like the achievements of an older artist who is ready to reflect on their lifetime's work, so it's hard to believe that Taylor already has all of this under her belt and is only in her fourth decade.

While writing this book, I've often thought about what would happen if we stored it all away like a time capsule and returned to it in 2053 – how many eras will there be then? What stories will Taylor be telling? Where will her life have taken her? And *how* will she be able to establish a setlist for another *Eras Tour* with at least 10 more albums thrown in there?

But forget the future for a second, as we're all here to celebrate Taylor Swift in *this* moment. As we prepare for however we're experiencing the *Eras Tour*, whether it's shimmying around in a white frill cotton dress and cowboy boots or donning our best Nineties grunge look, hopefully we've learned to be a little more like Taylor. Whether it be championing your pals at every possible opportunity, standing up for what you believe in and taking ownership of what's rightfully yours, following your dreams even when it feels impossible, or just referring to your cat as the love of your life, you are living your era, and learning that there's a reason why Taylor Swift is our role model.

Forever & Always,

Swifties everywhere

REFERENCES

INTRODUCTION
D'Souza, Shaad, '"She is a snake – in the most positive way!" How Taylor Swift Became the World's Biggest Pop Star, Again', *Guardian*, 8 September 2023.
Swift, Taylor, 'For Taylor Swift, Pop Is Personal', *Elle UK*, 28 February 2019.

CHAPTER 2: *FEARLESS (2008)*
Caramanica, Jon, 'My Music, Myspace, My Life', *New York Times*, 7 November 2008.
Gomez, Selena, as told to Rosenberg, Carissa of *Seventeen*, 20 October 2009.
Swift, Taylor, Twitter, 11 February 2021.
Swift, Taylor, MTV News, 2009.

CHAPTER 3: *SPEAK NOW (2010)*
Swift, Taylor, as told to Hiatt, Brian in 'Taylor Swift: The *Rolling Stone* Interview', 18 September 2019.
Swift, Taylor, *Speak Now* liner notes, 25 October 2010.
Swift, Taylor, as told to Willman, Chris in 'Princess Crossover', *New York Magazine*, 7 October 2010.
Sisario, Ben, 'Taylor Swift Album Is a Sales Triumph', 3 November 2010.
Werde, Bill, 'Taylor Swift Named Billboard Woman of the Year' by Schneider, Marc, 10 November 2011.
Swift, Taylor, Instagram, 2 December 2022.
Swift, Taylor, 'Taylor Swift on 60 Minutes', CBS News, November 2011.
Swift, Taylor, as told to Meltzer, Marisa in 'When Two Thumbs Down Are a Sign of Approval', *New York Times*, 9 August 2011.

CHAPTER 4: *RED (2012)*
Swift, Taylor, as told to Bernstein, Jonathan in '500 Greatest Albums: Taylor Swift Looks Back on Her "Only True Breakup Album"

"Red"', *Rolling Stone*, 18 November 2020.
Swift, Taylor, Instagram Live, 2019.
Swift, Taylor, 'Rolling Stone and Amazon Music's upcoming 500 Greatest Albums podcast', 27 October 2020.
Swift, Taylor, live web chat, August 2012.
Swift, Taylor, Instagram, 18 June 2021.
'Why Taylor Swift's "Red" Is Her Turning Point', *Clash*, 1 November 2021.
Pitchfork, 1 October 2021.
Nelson, Ivy, *Red* retrospective review, 19 August 2019.
Sargent, Jon, 'Listen to Taylor Swift's *Red*, One of the Best Pop Albums of Our Time', *Spin*, 16 June 2017.
Sheffield, Rob, '"Red (Taylor's Version)" Makes a Classic Even Better', *Rolling Stone*, 12 November 2021.
Swift, Taylor, Napster, 2012.
Swift, Taylor, '*Rolling Stone*'s 500 Greatest Albums podcast', 17 November 2020.
Swift, Taylor, PopDust, 2012.

CHAPTER 5: *1989 (2014)*
Antonoff, Jack, Instagram, 14 October 2014.
Swift, Taylor, '30 Things I Learned Before Turning 30', *ELLE*, 6 March 2019.
Swift, Taylor, as told to Iasimone, Ashley, 'Taylor Swift Interview: Changing Things Up With "1989" and Turning 25', PopCrush, 27 October 2014.
Borchetta, Scott, as cited by Light, Alan in '*Billboard* Woman of the Year Taylor Swift on Writing Her Own Rules, Not Becoming a Cliché and the Hurdle of Going Pop', *Billboard*, 12 May 2015.

CHAPTER 6: *reputation (2017)*
Swift, Taylor, as told to Agguire, Abby in 'Taylor Swift on Sexism, Scrutiny, and Standing Up for Herself', *Vogue*, 8 August 2019.
Swift, Taylor, as told to Suskind, Alex/ *Entertainment Weekly* in 'Taylor Swift

Reveals How Game of Thrones (and Arya's Kill List) Inspired reputation', Entertainment Weekly, 9 May 2019.

Swift, Taylor at a Taylor Swift Now concert in Chicago, 2018.

Swift, Taylor, University of Phoenix Stadium, Glendale, Arizona, 8 May 2018.

CHAPTER 7: Lover (2019)

Swift, Taylor, as told to Norton, Graham on The Graham Norton Show, 24 May 2019.

Swift, Taylor, as told to Agguire, Abby in 'Taylor Swift on Sexism, Scrutiny, and Standing Up for Herself', Vogue, 8 August 2019.

Caramanica, Jon, 'For Taylor Swift, Is Ego Stronger Than Pride?' New York Times, 8 June 2019.

Netflix, Miss Americana, 31 January 2020.

Swift, Taylor, Billboard Woman of the Decade acceptance speech, 12 December 2019.

Swift, Taylor, June 2023 Eras Tour stop.

Swift, Taylor, as told to Willman, Chris in 'Taylor Swift: No Longer "Polite at All Costs"', Variety, 21 January 2020.

CHAPTER 8: folklore (2020)

Swift, Taylor, Instagram, 23 July 2020.

Swift, Taylor, Instagram, 24 July 2020.

Reynolds, Ryan on SiriusXM, August 2021.

Swift, Taylor, Eras Tour, May 2023.

Swift, Taylor, YouTube, July 2020.

Bruner, Raiser, 'Let's Break Down Taylor Swift's Tender New Album Folklore', TIME, 24 July 2020.

Garrabrant, Beth, as told to Whitfield, Zoe in 'Meet the Photographer Behind Taylor Swift's folklore Artwork', i-D, 24 September 2020.

Swift, Taylor, as told to McCartney, Paul in 'Musicians on Musicians: Taylor Swift & Paul McCartney', Rolling Stone, 13 November 2020.

Willman, Chris, 'Taylor Swift's "Folklore": Album Review', Variety, 23 July 2020.

O'Connor, Roisin in 'Taylor Swift Review, Folklore: This Shimmering Album Is Exquisite,

Piano-based Poetry', Independent, 24 July 2020.

CHAPTER 9: evermore (2021)

Swift, Taylor, Instagram, 10 December 2020.

Dessner, Aaron, as told to Havens, Lyndsey in 'Aaron Dessner on the "Weird Avalanche" That Resulted in Taylor Swift's "Evermore"', Billboard, 18 December 2020.

Desnner, Aaron, Sound on Sound, March 2021

Swift, Taylor, as told to Zane Lowe on Apple Music, 16 December 2020.

Swift, Taylor, BRIT Awards, 11 May 2021.

King, Jason, Yankee Stadium, 18 May 2022.

Swift, Taylor, Yankee Stadium, 18 May 2022.

CHAPTER 10: Midnights (2022)

Swift, Taylor, Instagram, 29 August 2022.

Swift, Taylor, TikTok, 21 September 2022.

Swift, Taylor, Instagram, 21 October 2022.

Swift, Taylor, Instagram, 3 October 2022.

Swift, Taylor, YouTube, 8 October 2022.

Swift, Taylor, Twitter, 2 January 2023.

Swift, Taylor, Instagram, 12 October 2022.

Del Rey, Lana, as told to Robinson, Kristin in 'How Lana Del Rey Became "Completely Unburdened" for Her Most Personal Material Yet', Billboard, 24 February 2023.

Snapes, Laura, 'The 50 Best Albums of 2022', Guardian, 23 December 2022.

Cooper, John Mayor, 4 May 2023.

Nyce Nimbs, Caroline, 'Weirdly, Taylor Swift Is Extremely Close to Creating a True Metaverse', Atlantic, 21 October 2022.

Swift, Taylor, as told to Fallon, Jimmy on The Tonight Show Starring Jimmy Fallon, 22 November 2022.

Greenbaum, David and Greenfield, Matthew via Lee, Benjamin/Guardian in 'Taylor Swift to Direct Her First Feature-length Movie', Guardian, 9 December 2022.

PICTURE CREDITS

p94-5: Allen J. Schaben / Los Angeles Times via Getty Images; p13,72,79,80-1,112,119,128-9: Buda Mendes/TAS23/Getty Images for TAS Rights Management; p99: Christopher Polk/Penske Media via Getty Images; p19: Denise Truscello/WireImage/Getty Images; p86: Don Arnold/TAS18/Getty Images; pp36-7,133,157: Emma McIntyre/TAS23/Getty Images for TAS Rights Management; p30,35: Fabio Diena / Alamy Stock Photo; p1: Frederick M Brown/Getty Images; pp50-1: Hector Vivas/TAS23/Getty Images for TAS Rights Management; p105: imageSPACE/Shutterstock; p7: John Shearer/Getty Images for MTV/Paramount Global; p4,142,149: John Shearer/TAS23/Getty Images for TAS Rights Management; p69: Kevin Mazur/Wire Image/Getty Images; pp22-3: Kevin Winter/Getty Images for TAS Rights Management; pp14-5: Mark Humphrey/Associated Press/Alamy Stock Photo; p52,59: Nicky Loh/TAS/Getty Images for TAS; pp66-7: Sam Kovak / Alamy Stock Photo; p26: TAS Rights Management/Getty Images.

All illustrations by Amelia Deacon, with the exception of p4 (bottom), p41, p64: Shutterstock.com

All background textures: Shutterstock.com

HarperCollins*Publishers*
1 London Bridge Street
London SE1 9GF

www.harpercollins.co.uk

HarperCollins*Publishers*
Macken House, 39/40 Mayor Street Upper
Dublin 1, D01 C9W8, Ireland

First published by
HarperCollins*Publishers* 2024

10 9 8 7 6 5 4 3 2 1

© HarperCollins*Publishers* 2024

ISBN 978-0-00-868626-0

Printed and bound by GPS

MIX
Paper | Supporting
responsible forestry
FSC™ C007454

This book contains FSC™ certified paper
and other controlled sources to ensure
responsible forest management.

For more information visit: www.
harpercollins.co.uk/green